Dreams That Come True

Dreams That Come True

··

Barbara Garwell

*A medium's predictions from the past
and visions of the future*

Thorsons
An Imprint of HarperCollinsPublishers

Thorsons
An Imprint of HarperCollins*Publishers*
77–85 Fulham Palace Road,
Hammersmith, London W6 8JB
1160 Battery Street
San Francisco, California 94111–1213

Published by Thorsons 1996
1 3 5 7 9 10 8 6 4 2

©Barbara Garwell 1996

Barbara Garwell asserts the moral right
to be identified as the author of this work

A catalogue record for this book
is available from the British Library

ISBN 0 7225 3251 2

Printed in Great Britain by
HarperCollins Manufacturing Glasgow

Contents

Acknowledgements

I should like to thank all the people who contributed to the chapter of testimonials towards the end of this book; also thanks are due to Peter Mullen who helped with the writing.

Preface

It is possible to become enchanted in the 1990s – I know, it happened to me.

One evening in the autumn of 1994 I was looking at – to say watching would be to put it too strongly – the television when I saw a woman's face which struck me for its remarkable sincerity of expression. The programme was *Out of this World* and the woman was Barbara Garwell.

Barbara was talking to the interviewer about her successful predictions: the assassination of President Sadat, the death of John Lennon and the Windsor castle fire. I was impressed. And that was unusual because, as a journalist of many years, I am not easily beguiled by hype and sensationalism. But Barbara fascinated me because there was about her what I can only describe as the ring of truth.

The presenter on *Out of this World* said that Barbara lived in Hull, which is only an hour's drive from where I live in York. I thought to myself, 'All right. I'll call directory enquiries and see if she's on the 'phone. If so, I'll ring and ask for an interview and write it up for one of the newspapers.'

I had determined I was not going to chase the story very hard: if Barbara answered when I rang – good; if not – forget it. I can hardly say how pleased I am now that she did answer and agree to give me that interview.

I drove across to Hull and met Barbara and her husband Roland in their neat bungalow in a leafy suburb a mile or two away from the busy port and the North Sea ferries. This was the beginning of my enchantment. There was nothing weird or occult about Barbara. She made no attempt to whip up a sense of mystery for a journalist's sake. No exotic posing or fanciful chat.

Here was a kind-hearted, down-to-earth Yorkshire lady with a husband and family: an ordinary woman, you might say, to whom the most extraordinary things had happened – and continue to happen. She told me of her richly prophetic dreams and visions; but in our conversation I realised that these things were not the be-all and end-all of her existence.

Barbara Garwell is a fascinating person in her visions and out of them. Her prophecies are stunning. Her life is truly amazing. She is the genuine article – a real character: fascinating, warm-hearted, human. Her life is an inspiration.

As I drove back to York, I determined to help Barbara to tell her intriguing tale, to write her life story. This book is the result.

Peter Mullen
York 1995

1
...

Your Young Ones Shall See Visions

The school corridor was filled with dusty sunlight and the babble of children's voices. I was seven years old, my head full of skipping rhymes and only half as full of the times-tables as it ought to have been! It was St Patrick's Roman Catholic school and all the teachers were nuns. We were excited because it was the beginning of another year and we were being shown into our new classroom.

Sister Lucy shushed us and then, when we were silent, opened the door. It was a big move up from Infants to Juniors and the classroom looked almost too spacious for little girls. But as soon as I looked in at the door, I knew something with more certainty than I had ever known anything before. I knew at once which was my desk and I marched over to it and sat down. I must have appeared astonishingly bold – but I didn't feel bold ... just certain! Sister Lucy directed all the others to their seats and then she came to me:

'Barbara; who told you to sit there?'

'No one, Sister.'

I was a little afraid and I felt strange. Not afraid of Sister Lucy, but uneasy. I knew that something eerie and quite out of the ordinary had happened. Sister Lucy looked at me and smiled. I could see that she too was puzzled: half-puzzled, half-amused. I was only glad she was not angry with me in front of all the class – that would have been intolerable.

'Well,' she said, 'that's the desk I'd marked out for you right enough. Have you got magic powers or something? You'd better sit down again then.'

A small, childish event. It was my first psychic experience: the first time I ever encountered that shadow of premonition which was to come to me hundreds – no, thousands – of times over the following sixty years. What passes through a seven-year-old's mind at such a time? I was only concerned to get out into the playground and eat my apple.

All this happened in Hull, Yorkshire, where I was born on 27 July 1929. We lived at number one, Hill's Terrace, a little back-to-back house; a 'two up and two down'. My bedroom looked out over the back yard and there was an abattoir opposite. Steel, coal and the docks. A little grocer's shop called 'Greens' – as if it had been part of the Happy Families card game: Mr Green, the grocer. A newsagent's with a stern proprietress, thin and grey with a high-pitched, chiding voice. And Harmer's ice cream emporium where we bought our Sunday cornets.

I was a seventh child. My father too was a seventh child. And so was his mother. There is a tradition which says that such children inherit spiritual gifts.

I adored my father and I used to love to listen to his tales about his own early life. He was christened Harry – Harry Gill, born in Sheffield in 1885. His stories were like the *Arabian Nights* to me and my brothers and sisters: how he had run off to sea at the age of sixteen ... I can see him now, sitting in his chair in the corner and wagging his finger, saying, 'That was the year Queen Victoria died.'

When he was seventeen, he falsified his age and enlisted in the army. He was posted to India where he became a Lance Corporal and a medical orderly. He would sit us all down at bedtimes and tell us tales of

India, mysterious stories about the Taj Mahal. All told in a soft, lilting voice that made me excited and drowsy at the same time. And the hand gestures – as if describing the Indian rope trick.

In the First World War my father was wounded at the Somme. I am a bit hazy about the actual sequence of events from these early days, but I do know that a pal of my father – 'Uncle Wilf' – introduced him to Kathleen Allman, from Norwich, and that father married her in 1915.

I remember much more clearly a true story my father told me about how the troopship he was meant to have been on was torpedoed and blown to pieces. Father had missed the boat. A lucky accident? This was the first time I heard the expression 'Guardian Angel'. After the war, father and mother lived in Greenwich at first where father worked as a 'rougher' at Redpath-Brown Iron and Steel Foundry. The rougher's job was to feed the raw materials into the fire and then to shape them when they were molten. Their first child, my brother Frank, was born in Norwich and there is a story about how he walked the length of the Blackwall tunnel, aged two.

In the early 1920s, the family moved to Hull and my father got a job in the foundry there, again as a rougher. My eldest sister, Mary, was born in 1920. She was followed by Phyllis, 1923; Russell, 1924; Marjorie, 1926; Audrey, 1927; me in 1929 – the seventh child of a seventh child of a seventh child – Bernard, 1931; and Norman, 1934 completed the family.

I had what social workers today would call a hard, poverty-stricken, northern working-class upbringing. But it didn't seem like that to me. There was never much money, true enough, but my mother was a good household manager and father was hard-working and loyal. As well as the foundry work which was gruelling enough, he used to knit socks and dresses for my sisters and me. I never heard a cross word between him and my mother.

My sister Mary must have been a magic child. Aged only eight or nine, she had got to know all the local shopkeepers and she would negotiate the best prices. I remember little of her, but all I have heard makes me think of her as almost saintly. What is the saying about those whom the gods love dying young?

But this is strange. When Mary was only two, my father's mother told my mother that she would die when she was twelve. And she did die – of tubercular meningitis. I was only three at the time so I remember nothing of it. But my sister Marjorie was lifted up to see her in her coffin in the front room and she just screamed and screamed.

Such lovely long black hair Mary had. I remember my mother crying. A woman in the street said, 'You won't miss Mary: you've got four other girls.' My mother came into the house. She cried and cried.

When I was ten, I saw my dead sister alive. In the bedroom I shared with my sisters there was a tall wardrobe. I saw through the wardrobe door, as if it had not been there. It was my sister Mary. I know it was. Such lovely long black hair. I asked my other sisters if they had seen anything. 'Nothing at all,' they said.

Many times in my life, people have asked me where I got my psychic gift. Did I ask for it? In fact, I never asked for it. I never even knew that it was a psychic gift. These things just came to me. I could not deny them. They simply happened and they became a part of my life. I used to say to my father: 'Why can't I knit neatly? Why am I so bad at blackboard sums?'

He just said, 'Other little girls haven't got what you've got. You have other talents. Wait and see.'

How did he know? What did he know? One thing for

sure is that is that he was psychically gifted as well. He used to interpret our dreams for us, and he would read my mother's fortune in the tea leaves. I used to say, 'But you can't see anything in the cup, father. It's just leaves.'

He said, 'The pictures aren't in the leaves, you're right. They're symbols. As I concentrate on the leaves – then I see things. You see, they're only the means of seeing.' Almost at once I seemed to catch his meaning and I found that I could tell fortunes from the leaves too.

I remember also that 'Aunt' Maud would come visiting. She wasn't really an aunt but just a friend of the family. She was plump, white-haired and she brought her cards to the house and told my mother's fortune. It was the age before television and video games. A pack of cards – the colours, the strange expressions on the faces of the court cards – it was mysterious, magical to a young child.

When the Second World War broke out, my father, being too old for the armed forces, became an emergency firewatcher and night-watchman. He was stationed at the local undertaker's. One night I was lying in bed when I 'saw' my father and I knew at once that he was in great peril. It was so vivid: light and fire and noise. I screamed and tore my hair – woke up the whole house. 'Whatever's the matter, girl?' my mother asked.

'It's father. He's in danger. I know he is!' He was late home. The undertaker's had received a direct hit. He was lucky to be alive.

'Your young men shall see visions and your old men shall dream dreams.' I read those words in the family Bible. I was neither a young man nor an old man, only a girl. But I was both dreaming dreams and seeing visions. Was something trying to prevent the visions, disable me or even kill me? I have asked myself this question often because, no fewer than five times between the ages of five and eleven, I fell on the back of my head and had to have it stitched – always in the same place.

I left school at the age of fourteen. It was wartime and I went to work at Needlers chocolate factory in Hull. I was a 'dipper' – dipping the eclairs in the chocolate from six in the morning until six in the evening for 'seventeen and a tanner' (87.5p) per week. I was very proud of my eclairs!

Hull is a port and therefore it was a target for the bombers. My Aunt Nell – mother's sister – lived in Newark in Nottinghamshire and I suppose she got round to thinking that the little market town would be a safer place for a teenage girl. Also, she was not very well and she really needed some help about the house. Her husband was a retired warrant officer and he had become a subpostmaster.

So I went to Newark to help Aunt Nell. I learned everything there was to know about postal orders and stamps and I helped around the house. I suppose my aunt and uncle were quite well off. Certainly they were a lot better placed than any of us in Hull. I could have anything I wanted. They were so kind, having no children of their own. But I was homesick and I used to brood.

One day – it was a hot day in June – I told Aunt Nell I was going for a walk and that I would not be longer than half an hour. I wandered down the lane and past the main road which ran beside the barracks. I always used this road as a landmark so I knew I couldn't get lost. But strangely – it was June, remember – a thick mist came down and, as I walked, I very soon had no idea of my whereabouts.

I was still brooding, feeling homesick and sad. I wandered on and on in the mist, for further than I had ever intended. Suddenly, I felt something or someone pulling on my left arm and I heard a voice call out of the fog: 'Stop! That's far enough.'

I stopped dead in my tracks. One pace more and I would have fallen into the river. That was amazing enough but equally amazing was that I found my way back to Aunt Nell's house though the fog at no time lifted. 'Wherever have you been? You've been gone two and a half hours!' Where had I been indeed? It had seemed to me like only twenty minutes or so.

For all my aunt and uncle's kindness, I was unhappy at Newark and after six months I returned to the family in Hull. I had earned £65. A princely sum in 1943. And I had, thanks to my uncle and aunt's generosity, saved every penny.

Words came back to me: 'guardian angels'. I knew that my Guardian Angel had saved me from the river. I was baptised in the Catholic faith and I have practised my religion all my life. People sometimes ask me how I reconcile the strange visions and intuitions which I have received with Catholic teaching, thinking the Church is against all that sort of thing.

There has never been a moment's doubt in my mind: the gift – if that is what it is – is from God. There is nothing occult or magical about it. I don't know why it was given to me, except sometimes I have been able to use it for good, to warn people of disasters. I shall tell you about those occasions later but for the present I am content to describe my early years when the visions were surprising to me also. People think that those who have the psychic gift must be able to explain it. Well I cannot. It has simply been a part of my life from the earliest days and it is not something which I can influence one way or the other. Like the old gifts in fairy stories it sometimes seems like a blessing but it can also feel like a curse – especially when what I foresee turns out to be disastrous.

I had already been caused physical pain on account of my visions. The night when I had seen my father in great peril at his fire-watching in the undertaker's, I had become so terrified that he might be dead that I had cried out again and again hysterically. My mother slapped my face really hard.

The gift brought me emotional pain too. I remember thinking, 'Oh please God don't let my father be killed! I love him so! What would I do without my father?' The agony was intense, and all the time it was as if I was seeing hell break loose and my father's cap on the back of the door.

The feelings, the emotional sensations, which accompany my premonitions are extremely intense and I know that some psychologists have tried to explain everything away, visions and the like, as by-products of sexuality. Put it all down to hormones, even! It is a well-known fact that some experts have associated poltergeists with the awakening sexual feelings of teenage girls, for example. Well, I don't know anything about that and I wouldn't want to make pronouncements one way or the other. All I know is what has happened to me. I have received hundreds of visionary experiences and many of these have come true. As for the explanation of all this – I leave explanations to the 'experts'. I am simply recording honestly what I have seen, what has been shown to me.

I have a very clear recollection of the next premonition which I received in 1945 when I was fifteen. I awoke at 2am with the sensation that I was in Northern Ireland. An aeroplane was nosediving. A frightful din. An ear-shattering screaming of engines. I didn't actually see the aircraft hit the ground.

The next things I saw were dead bodies partly covered under hessian cloth. A voice said out loud, 'Eighty bodies'. Strangely – it seemed like a black comedy – I then saw three men in the cockpit and over their heads was a rugby ball. In the morning I told my father all about what I had seen.

There was nothing in the papers about a plane crash. I remember it was a Sunday. Then, on the one o'clock news, it was announced: a plane had crashed in Northern Ireland and eighty people had been killed.

I cried out to my father, 'But the survivors, what about the survivors?'

He said, 'There's nothing about any survivors!'

'But there must be. I saw them! There are three survivors.'

And so it turned out. Three of them. The plane passengers had been to a rugby match. I had seen a rugby ball above the heads of the survivors.

I want to stress that I did not go through these early years with a sense of being haunted; a 'special' child. I generally felt absolutely normal and I had the usual friendships – and boyfriends – as anyone does. There was no sense of being chosen or singled out. It was simply the case that, from time to time, I was given to see and know things which others did not know until later.

When I was in the middle of one of these experiences the atmosphere was strange, even frightening. But for the rest of the time I was an ordinary girl lucky enough to have been born into a loving and happy family and surrounded by the usual quota of friends and acquaintances. I was neither particularly brilliant at school nor especially stupid, but one aspect of my abilities – or the lack of them – puzzled me and it still does. When sums in fractions or long-division were written up on the blackboard, I used to quake because I could never work them out by the prescribed, mechanical methods. But I found I sometimes 'knew' the correct answers in my head. I claim no credit for this because I have no idea how it all worked. Just sometimes I seemed to know the answers at once.

'You must become as a little child,' it says in the Bible. What does that mean? My childhood was ordinary and extremely happy. I loved school. I pleaded with the Headteacher, Sister Mary Rita, that I might not have to leave. But of course she was powerless to keep me at school when the time came for me to leave. If I'm honest, I have to say I never really wanted to grow up.

My childhood was a magical time: not magic in the weird or occult sense. But we were such a close family and I was surrounded with love. It was a whole world really – even if it was a world with bare boards and rugs hanging on the wall to dry; when sometimes we could only afford a single bucket of coal at tuppence – less than 1p in today's coinage!

My father wasn't a Catholic at first but he agreed that we children should be brought up in the faith. And eventually he converted. We went to Mass every Sunday, and I do so still. I have sometimes thought to myself after a particularly striking premonition: 'Be careful, Barbara – the Church used to burn witches!' But it isn't like that. There is no malevolent force behind any of my strange experiences. I know that to be true.

The dreams and visions turned out to be not things that belonged to childhood, things I would grow out of. They continued. In fact they intensified and became more frequent and more specific after my marriage in 1951 to Roland Garwell, an electrician and my lifelong love and companion.

2
...

The Darkness and the Dawning

1951 came cold and grey in Hull and there were gales and floods all down the east coast of England. Sometimes you felt you were living under a wet tarpaulin. The six years since the end of the war had been a time of austerity and shortages, of make do and mend. Now at last, in 1951, there were signs of recovery and there was a new cheerfulness in the air. It was the year of The Festival of Britain on the south bank of the Thames and there was a sense of optimism. As a nation we were about to throw away the ration books.

It was a memorable year for me: on 24 March, at St Patrick's Church in Spring Street, Roland and I were married. We decided not to try to find a place of our own, because Roland was due to be called up for his National Service and it would have been no fun for me to begin married life living on my own. So we lived at my mother's house. Roland was summoned to Catterick Camp on 8 June.

His life sounded a lot more exciting than mine: he was a dispatch rider in the Royal Signals. I helped out in Roland's parents' off-licence shop which was only a few streets away from where I lived. The shop stocked other goods apart from drink – there were pills and potions, proprietary medicines, bottles and jars of this and that: all good old-fashioned home remedies. One of my jobs was to fill these bottles and jars, and it was while doing this that I repeatedly had a strong sense of déjà vu. I had only to stand on the chair and begin restocking those shelves to experience indubitably that I had done the job somewhere else ... another time, another place, you might say; but in reality I hadn't.

I know now that this experience was just a part of my general psychic sensitivity; but I didn't know it at the time. I got these strange, eerie feelings and I had no means of telling what they meant. Did everyone get these sorts of sensations? How could I know? I was a young woman of twenty-two and, I suppose, fairly naive by the world's standards of sophistication.

A strange thing: while Roland was in the army, I always got a premonition about his movements. If he was to be transferred to another billet or military depot, I would receive a dream or a waking vision of him standing on a station platform with his kit bag. Two or three days later I would get his letter in the post: 'Dear Barbara, We are being moved to so-and-so ...'

My great joy at this time was the discovery that I was pregnant. Well, I have already said that my psychic gift was inherited through my father, and one day around this time I asked him to read my tea cup. He read it and his face was at once creased with shadows. 'What does it say?' I asked.

He shook his head. Three times I asked him, and he replied, 'Don't make me, Barbara.'

I pressed him and at last he said, 'I'm reluctant to speak.' He did speak – like a man unburdening himself of an intolerable weight. 'You'll have a girl,' he said. 'I see an operating theatre and a bed with a green covering and two surgeons – one of them with sparse, gingerish hair. But don't ask me to tell you any more ...'

Of course, I did ask. He was like a man in agony. He said, 'But the 8th ...' That was all: 'But the 8th ...'

Our daughter was born at the end of November. It was not an easy birth, a forceps delivery. Still, everything seemed fine and we were all overjoyed. Roland, home on leave, brought me anemones. You have to remember that we were comparatively ignorant of medical procedures in those days and so I did not immediately imagine anything to be amiss when I was not sent with the other mothers to learn how to wash my baby. I suppose I just thought my turn would come in due course, and meanwhile I trusted that all was well.

But my sleep was interrupted by a sinister and frighteningly atmospheric dream. I dreamt I was at my mother's house. I came along the landing and to the bottom of the step, from where I looked into the living room. I was holding out my arms – as if carrying a child – but my arms were empty. In the dream, my brother, a railway fireman, was sitting in my father's chair – a most unusual thing for him to do. As I approached, he said, 'Don't cry. We'll send for Roland.'

I awoke distraught.

Then, in real life, the Sister on the maternity ward said that my baby would have to go into hospital. She asked me what I would call my daughter, and I said her name should be Angela. I went home and I was collected every day in an ambulance to take milk, which I supplied through the breast-pump, to my sick child.

The Consultant Surgeon appeared on the scene and I shuddered. He was Mr Walton – a man with sparse, gingerish hair. He explained: 'Your daughter was born with a tangled bowel, and it's my job to untangle it. It can be done, and I will do it. But it is a serious operation. If Angela survives for three days after the op, she will recover.'

I had never seen my little girl with her eyes open.

One morning, my mother and I went to the hospital.

Angela was in an oxygen tent. I just looked at her. You can imagine ...

Then my little baby opened her eyes – just the once. As if to say, 'I've seen my mother, and that's fine!' Anyhow, that was the strong feeling I had at the time.

My sister Marjorie phoned very late to say Angela had died just before midnight. It was 8 December. I went into the living room at my mother's and my brother, the fire-man, was sitting there in father's chair, just as I had seen him in my dream. He spoke the same words: 'We'll send for Roland!'

Not long after these awful events, I was on my way out when, at the last minute, I decided to go back upstairs for a cardigan which I knew I had left on the pink basket chair in the bedroom. Suddenly, I saw a large blue light. It was lovely. It seemed to radiate peace and love. It rested on my arm. I knew it was Angela, letting me know that everything was all right. Also, around this time, I began to see a vision of her in her cot by my bed. In all these things, my psychic experiences were not frightening but it was as if they had been sent as a comfort and a reassur-ance to me.

Life, as it does, went on. Roland was demobilised from the army in 1953 and his parents gave us £50 which we were able to put down on a small terraced house: 1 Egton Villas, Hull. It is still standing today. Our daughter Linda was born in August 1954; and Sandra followed in November the next year – on Bonfire Night.

It was a happy house, full of wonderful presences. When I was on my own I used to hear women's voices whispering musically in the bedroom. It was like a secret garden. Whispered melodies from the four corners. It was lovely. Roland got a good job as an electrician at the local oil and cake mills and we were very happy.

I must stress again that my psychic awareness did not

come to me fully developed in a way that I could instantly understand. It was a slowly dawning mystery to me – and to some extent it still is. Strange, out-of-the-ordinary experiences would happen and it was only much later that I came to understand their significance. I was psychic right enough: I know that now, but I didn't know it then. However gifted a psychic might be, he or she may not have complete understanding of the gift. It is a bit like swimming or riding a bike: you can do it, but you don't know, quite, how you do it – and the more you think about it, or try to manage it, the more volatile and elusive it becomes.

One such strange experience happened while my daughters were young. My sister Audrey invited me for a week's stay with her in Romford. It was to be a break from the children. Audrey's mother-in-law was a Spiritualist and she asked me to attend a service at her church. This was taboo to me, a traditional Catholic. But Audrey's mother-in-law said, 'All religions are irrelevant in these matters. Just come along and see.'

So I went. It wasn't at all like any church I had been used to: it was a huge hall, sort of municipal on the grand scale. And it was packed. The lady speaker was giving spirit messages to various members of the congregation. There was no message for me, but after the service she came to me informally and she said, 'I didn't give you your message – but in the years to come you will have dreams and premonitions. You'll speak to people and help them, and your psychic ability will grow.'

I was faintly embarrassed by what she had said, and I scarcely believed or even understood her. But when I returned to Hull, I received a striking confirmation of the truth of what that lady in Romford had indicated. I was in a queue at the *Hull Daily Mail* offices in order to pay a bill. Suddenly, I noticed that the woman clerk on the counter had a sort of glow around her head – not quite a halo, as it were. I now realise that this was in fact what Spiritualists and psychics call the aura. Everyone has his own aura – a truth well-attested by parapsychologists – though, of course, I did not know at the time.

This I find to be one of the most convincing confirmations of the veracity of my psychic gift: that I repeatedly experienced such things before I had any inkling that these sorts of experiences were part of the repertoire of what has come to be described as the paranormal. The truth was that the lady speaker in Romford had opened up channels in my mind and my psychic awareness was developing, as she had said it would.

I will digress here to make an important point. Psychic experiences are not always deeply serious. There is often a sense of light-heartedness and even fun or humour involved. Once, for example, I had been asked to appear on a television programme dealing with the paranormal. I was with the Producer in a restaurant when the waiter, overhearing snippets of our conversation, I suppose, exclaimed, 'So you're psychic! Can you tell me anything?'

I said, 'Yes. You're going to have trouble with your feet.' He laughed at this, but a couple of weeks later he rang to say he had had to visit the chiropodist! There is a happy little incident to round off this story. The waiter kept in touch with me, and one day he phoned in some torment to ask if his relationship with his girlfriend – with whom he was deeply in love – could be repaired. They had had some cataclysmic fall-out. I saw clearly that they would get together again and be very happy; and so I was able to reassure him. It's nice when you have the chance to do something like that.

I have been able on many occasions to tell people things about their personal future and I shall recount some of these stories later. But sufficient for now to say that what the Spiritualist lady said to me in Romford was beginning to come true: people were asking me questions and I was, now and then, able to help them.

In 1959 Roland got a new job at Blackburn Aircraft. Twenty pounds a week was a lot of money in those days! We thought of ourselves as really well-off. His father died that year, and on the night he died I saw the whole of one side of the bedroom in a swiftly moving mist. I knew that it was Roland's father – his spirit moving into the nearer presence of God.

I said that I felt sure the Spiritualist lady had awakened things in me. I have also often had the experience of awakening spirits and presences in houses which Roland and I have lived in. Roland would be the last person to claim any psychic abilities for himself, but this is what once happened.

Blackburn Aircraft were on strike and so money was short. I got a job at Jackson's Bakery to help with the household budget. One evening I returned from work to find Roland standing at the garden gate in a condition of great anxiety. 'Thank goodness you've come home!' he said, 'I'm so scared. I saw the kettle lift off the cooker and begin to pour – all on its own accord'. He would not go back into the house until I agreed to go in with him. He was, after that, always all right when I was in the house with him – but not otherwise. I know that I had awakened certain presences in the place. I know because it has happened again and again.

We sold that house and bought a shop – sweets, tobacco, a few groceries and that sort of thing. Roland's mother came to live with us and to help with the girls. We were always such good friends – the occasional tiff, but nothing serious. We didn't stay there long but moved in order to be closer to Roland's work. Out new house was near a railway track. There was a secluded garden. It was idyllic, and I loved it.

But one day I heard a voice say, 'You're not for here!' Instantly the whole atmosphere of the place changed for me and I knew I could never be happy there. Moreover, I soon knew where I was meant to be: that was with my father who was dying of cancer of the larynx. He was seventy-six.

Not long before he died, father said to me when we were alone: 'He'll be dressed in black, and he'll come for me. But I'm not afraid.' While I was sitting on the settee with my father, I saw a man in black, in a morning suit with a satin top hat and a ribbon. He was smiling. Father died shortly after that. He was baptised a Catholic only six weeks before his death. I was with him and he had a beautiful vision of his daughter – my sister Mary, who had died aged twelve – who came to take him to heaven.

Psychic experiences are not occult and terrifying. They are for our comfort – to reassure us that this life is not all there is and death is not the end. They are not contradictory to ordinary experience or even to scientific understanding. They don't rule anything out, but are an extra dimension just as real – more so sometimes – as the world of sight and touch. The ordinary world and the psychic world are the same place, for they are together God's creation. The spiritual world is not unreal or shadowy. It's just that some people are privileged to see more of the whole than others. This is not through any special worth or intelligence – I would never claim those things for myself. It is quite simply a gift. And, like all true gifts, it comes unasked for, unbidden.

But with psychic gifts there is always a cost. In the spiritual economy, nothing is ever for nothing: insight and enlightenment are often accompanied by shadows and darkness. I was about to learn the truth of this in a savage and terrifying way. I thought I was losing my mind.

Here I was, a happily married young woman with a family – a woman who knew that, in some ill-defined and only half-realised way, she had some sort of spiritual gift which set her apart from other women of her own age. But I didn't make a thing of it or dwell on it. There were other things going on in my life – not least looking after a husband and two young children – and I didn't have the time to become preoccupied with my psychic experiences, even if I had wanted to. And I didn't want to. I was an ordinary person living a family life in a town in the north of England; interested in what ordinary people are interested in, and with my own small group of affectionate friends. I had no wish to make a profession out of the strange insights which now and then came my way.

Suddenly, though, I was stricken. I can find no other words to describe what happened to me. We moved to a house in Thoresby Street in Hull, and I began to see black-clock beetles in the street. Then I began to see them in the house. Some of these beetles were real, but others lurked in my imagination. They began to obsess me. The local council sent their pest-control man and he sprayed everywhere. Still I was obsessed with these beetles and I developed a full-blown phobia about them. I went to the doctor and he gave me some tranquillizers.

Now I understand what all this was about. It was, in medical terms, an obsessive-compulsive disorder attached to a phobia – like a phobic reaction to spiders or open spaces or being closed-in. The compulsive aspect showed itself in my insistence on washing my daughters' dresses five or six times a day if I thought they had touched a wall or a piece of pavement that had been anywhere near a black-clock beetle. They must have thought their mother was going mad. For a time, I thought I was mad!

We moved again, to Woodlands Road this time, and I got into the habit of going for a repeat prescription of my tranquillizers. I was in the house, unwrapping my new packet of tranquillizers, when I heard a voice say with great firmness, 'Throw them away!' I knew I needed these tablets badly, and I knew I would suffer if I threw them away. But I knew also that I had to obey the voice: it spoke with authority, and I knew it spoke for my own good.

I did suffer: two weeks of agonizing withdrawal symptoms. But then I was free. I took no more tranquillizers and my terror of beetles had evaporated. It is only now, thirty years later, that I can fully understand that frightening episode in my life when I thought I was losing my sanity. The phobia and the obsession-compulsion were a test and a challenge at the time when my psychic gift was emerging to full power.

I know now that those who are given a special gift are also called to suffer for it. I don't know, though, why it works like this, but it does. The lives of mystics and clairvoyants through the ages – people far more spiritually-gifted that I – were frequently beset by mental and spiritual bothers and problems. These were tests and challenges to their gifts. Even Our Lord himself suffered the darkness of his encounter with Satan in the temptations in the wilderness before he began his ministry.

I can, at this distance, interpret what happened to me at that scary and disorientating time. Something was trying to destroy my psychic gift, or, failing that, to render me so unbalanced that I would be incapable of putting it to good purpose. You can call this dark force the Devil if that is the sort of phraseology which makes sense to you. It may have been only the dark side of my own self trying its best to upset things. We all have such a dark side: it is the chaotic voice of selfishness and self-will. The voice I heard telling me to throw away the tablets was the antidote to my dark imaginings; and, thank God, it won the struggle.

I look at it like this. My gift was in the area of premonition, that is, it was to do with time. So the darkness which would try to destroy this gift showed me everywhere black clocks!

The obsession with the black-clock beetles was my dark night of the soul – an experience which I now know I had to go through before my psychic gift could come to full maturity. It's easy to say this now – obvious, even. But, believe me, there was nothing obvious about it at the time. I was growing inwardly, learning and developing. I could not see the emerging picture. My understanding of my gift was very slight, in its infancy.

I should have known. I should have remembered the old, true saying: 'The darkest hour is the one before the dawn'.

3
...

A Delayed Miracle and the
Death of a Princess

I have often been asked to explain how I can reconcile my psychic gift with my Roman Catholic faith. I can only repeat that I see no contradiction in these two things: all spiritual gifts come from God. But an actual example of this reconciliation of faith and foresight is better than a thousand arguments in favour of it. I can offer many striking accounts of my faith acting in combination with my psychic gift.

One morning during the war, when I was in my teens, my father was extremely angry over breakfast with my brother Bernard for a misdemeanour. It was time to go to work, so there was no opportunity for him to discipline Bernard there and then. Father had been known to get very fierce with Bernard on occasions and I was in dread of the chastisement that he might be in for when father came home in the evening. Not that he was ever brutal, but I feared a scene and an oppressive atmosphere.

This was on my mind through the day at school and eventually I plucked up courage to ask one of the sisters to let me go across to church to pray that father would not be too angry with Bernard. When I arrived in church, it was during the forty-hour exposition of the Blessed Sacrament. I knelt and looked at the Sacrament and there I saw Christ's face on it, and a crown of thorns. I prayed for father and Bernard – that there would be no trouble.

That evening when father came home he excused

Bernard for the wrong that he had done – a most unusual thing for father to do, for he was always strict in the imposition of punishment for wrongdoing. This was the first exception to his strict rule. It was also the first time I had seen the vision of Christ's face on the Blessed Sacrament. I have seen it ever since, every time there is a Solemn Exposition.

This is surely an unusual part of my psychic gift. But it is a holy thing too, a Catholic thing; and this is what reassures me that there is no contradiction, no rivalry, between the gift and my faith as a Catholic. Something further reassures me – I never asked to receive a vision of Our Lord's face; I never expected to receive such a vision. Much later, when I had grown up, I learned the truth that spiritual gifts come unbidden and usually when the recipient is least expecting them – when he or she is thinking about something (or someone) else entirely. My mind was certainly elsewhere: it was on my brother.

There is another common misconception about people who have a psychic gift. It is often thought that such people must be very clever and have all sorts of advanced kinds of knowledge. This is certainly not the case with me! My gift is just something which came to me and which I know I possess; but as to how it works I am completely ignorant. Frequently I have experiences which I recognise as definitely psychic but for which I have neither explanation nor interpretation.

For example, our daughter Linda was slow at learning to walk and Roland and I were concerned about her. One day when she was fifteen months old, and still not walking confidently, we looked down at her in her cot. Suddenly, her face changed to that of Roland's grandmother who was an old lady of seventy-eight. It stayed like this for no more than three seconds. But it was not an illusion. We both saw the phenomenon. This experience highlights another aspect of psychic awareness: sometimes it seems as if it is almost catching. Roland, who does not usually have these sorts of experiences, was in no doubt as to what he saw on this occasion. How? Why? Once again, I have no answer. Not long after this incident Linda began to walk confidently.

I firmly believe that psychic gifts are often connected somehow to other sorts of emotional disturbances and difficulties, and in the last chapter I described my neurotic horror of black-clock beetles. I am convinced that this irrational fear of mine was some sort of test or trial that was all bound up with the psychic events which were beginning to surround me.

Catholics claim that all things work together for good for those who love God; and I believe that even a fear or a neurosis can work God's good purposes. For instance, when our daughter Sandra was three years old her face swelled and she developed a bull-neck. The poor child was paralysed. The paediatrician diagnosed a severe kidney disease and Sandra was in and out of hospital for two years.

At last the kidney complaint abated but it left her with rheumatoid arthritis and we were told that she was unlikely ever to walk properly. She was treated with powerful steroids and had to wear splints on her arms and legs. To look at the little girl was enough to break your heart. I used to take her out in one of those long wheelchairs in which the patient reclines parallel with the ground.

The paediatrician, Dr Philpott, and our parish priest, Father Plunkett, agreed that Sandra might benefit from a pilgrimage to Lourdes. I remember clear as day Dr Philpott saying to me, 'Do you believe in miracles, Barbara?' I had no hesitation in replying, 'Oh yes!'

'Then you should take her,' he said.

Top Mum and Dad, circa 1957. Relaxing away from them all.
Above Linda and Jon, 1970. The smile that shows sisterly love.

Top Barbara aged 7. Afraid of the unknown.
Above Daughters Linda and Sandra with niece Diane.

Top Roland and myself 1945. Love's young dream looking to the future.
Above Barbara at Marsascale Church, Malta, 1985.

Top Roland and Barbara's
wedding day, 1951. Their
happiest day.
Left Barbara (bottom left)
with her sisters Marjorie
(top right) and Audrey
(bottom right) with their
mother (top left).
Right Roland and Barbara
outside one of their many
abodes, 1989.

Top Barbara with daughter Linda, 1954. Happiness comes from heaven above.
Above Barbara and Roland showing their more serious side, 1948.

Top Brother Frank
with sister Mary
(who died aged 12)
1924.
Below Aunt Nell with
Barbara's daughter
Linda and son Paul,
1962.
Middle Roland, 1951.
There's something
about a soldier.

Top Barbara is on the extreme right. Back row, first left: eldest sister Phyllis with youngest brother Norman. Back row, fourth from left: sister Marjorie. Front row, middle: sister Audrey. Front row, third from right: brother Bernard.

Below Aunt Nell with Barbara's daughters Sandra, left, and Linda, right.

Top Roland and Barbara with second daughter Linda, 1954.
Below Roland and Barbara on their 43rd anniversary, 1994.

Of course, I said I would go. What I did not tell Dr Philpott or Father Plunkett was that I was terrified of flying and I swore no one would ever get me up in the air! I went ahead and booked the trip and tried my best to persuade myself to overcome my neurotic fear. It was embarrassing as I kept booking and cancelling the flight as my mood rose and fell.

I prayed about this constantly, and I seemed to be told to go and see my aunt Nell who was living temporarily in Scunthorpe where she looked after the two noisy young sons of a working relative. It was the end of May when I went to visit her – a beautiful day – and Nell was in the garden. I could see she was in some distress. I went to her. She flung her arms around me and cried: 'I've just asked God to take me away from this place and those noisy boys and you've come!'

Aunt Nell was seventy-four. I begged her, 'Will you take our daughter to Lourdes for me?' She said she would and she did. At that moment I knew that Nell needed to go to Lourdes herself, and it was my neurosis which was giving her the opportunity which otherwise she would not have had.

As I said Dr Philpott had asked if I believed in miracles. We received a miracle – a delayed miracle. Against all the medical prognoses, Sandra was discharged from hospital able to walk properly when she was sixteen years old. Now she is married with three boys of her own.

How do I know this was a miracle and not just a matter of gradual, natural improvement in her condition? In 1987, Sandra had to go to hospital for a dental appointment. She was called by Dr Brocklehurst, the anaesthetist. He called for her, naturally, by her married name. He was astonished when she went forward: 'But you can't be Sandra Bradley,' he exclaimed, 'With these records you could never be out of a wheelchair!'

All the time that I was bringing up my family, my psychic gift was developing but I did not have the time or the inclination to attend to it in any analytical sort of way. From time to time things of an inexplicable nature just seemed to happen and, because most of my time and energies were spent in the home, these things were mainly domestic, concerning the family.

One day in 1966, the girls were getting ready to go back to school for the afternoon when I heard terrible cries and screams, but there was no one making this dreadful noise. Moments later there was another scream, and this time it was Linda who had caught her finger in the back door on her way out. She shrieked and I don't wonder: the tip of her finger was severed in the accident.

How domestic can psychic experiences get? One year Roland was very ill. He suffered an attack of viral meningitis and was in hospital. Around this time, my brother bought a big friendly, black and white sheepdog called Whisky. Linda was fifteen and she had a Saturday job. One Saturday Whisky followed her as she set off to work. The dog was knocked down and killed. Exactly one year later, I was awakened in the night by a vision of that dog. I stroked it then and on three other occasions. And when I say I stroked it, I don't mean that I imagined I was stroking some sort of ghostly image of a dog: it was a real, tangible dog which came to me in the night, and I really stroked him.

In 1970 our son John was born. He was unusual in that he definitely had some sort of spiritual connection with his sister Angela whom he had, of course, never seen. He seemed to belong in Angela's period somehow. One day, on the anniversary of Angela's death, I went to put a posy of anemones on her grave. John came with me. He suddenly stopped in his tracks in the cemetery and said, 'There's a voice. It's like angels. It's Angela's voice!'

On another occasion John called me into his bedroom where he said he could see a smiling lady. He was not afraid. I couldn't see this lady, so I said, 'Tell me about her. What's she like?' He described her and added, 'She's picking up a scarf and putting it on. She's pulling it tight – like this'. He completed the gesture. It was the action of my mother whom John had never seen.

Sometimes a psychic insight is a fleeting thing which seems to come from nowhere and go back to nowhere all in an instant. The impression is powerful and unmistakable nonetheless, and it lingers like a haunting. I know that it is significant but I don't know quite why it is significant. Then sometimes the meaning becomes clear later. For example, one night I was sitting by the fire when I saw a vision in the fire of a dead cardinal. It startled me. The next day there was an account in the paper of a prominent cardinal who had died.

I know for certain that psychics have an unspoken attraction to one another which amounts to something like recognition. This happens without the need for formal introductions of any kind. I was once on Southend pier when an Indian gentleman came up to me and announced, out of the blue, 'You will have relatives in Australia one day!' Thirty years later my brother went to live there.

This and similar experiences make me reflect on the nature of psychic awareness. Perhaps we should not speak of such awareness as something which a person possesses at all. It is rather as if these psychic perceptions are hanging around in the air waiting to be perceived; but unlike ordinary physical perceptions they are not perceived by everyone. I am not advancing this as a scientific explanation; it is just how these things seem sometimes to me.

There are no guarantees that the psychic perceptions

will be agreeable. Sometimes they are horrific, full of foreboding and signifying tragedy. I have had to learn to accept this as a fact. In any case it is not something over which I have any control.

Perhaps there isn't always a purpose to these events. Maybe some incidences of psychic perception are simply but mysteriously a sort of telescoping of time – time present and time future. We have access to the past, after all, through the faculty of memory; and the memory creates its own vivid pictures. Perhaps we should regard premonitions as a sort of memory-in-advance. Time, it seems to me, is irrelevant. If something happens, it is real. Why should reality not be foreseen as well as remembered?

Now and then a psychic experience is personally poignant and the feeling is of being granted or given a privilege or dispensation – a kind of grace. I once felt a strong compulsion that I must see again my old head-mistress whom I loved. This was Sister Mary Rita. I went to the convent but I was told that Mary Rita was in retreat and that she could therefore see no one. A voice said, 'If you want to see her, it's now or never!' So I pleaded with the authorities and they relented and let me see her. I took her narcissuses and daffodils. It was lovely to see her again. Three days later, she died. It had truly been 'now or never'.

In this chapter I have mainly recorded psychic experiences of a personal and family nature, but around this time my premonitions began to be more public and specific. It was almost as if I had completed a kind of apprenticeship and now I was ready to see things which went beyond the family circle – though of course I had had one or two experiences of this sort before, such as the plane crash involving the rugby players.

In 1971, for three nights in succession, I had a vision

of a fire blazing behind rows of Georgian windows and I 'heard' fire-engine, police and ambulance sirens. The following night this all happened for real as a factory and paint works in Hull caught fire.

All these were domestic or local events but now the mood changes. I should like to tell you about a spectacular and haunting vision which I had in 1982 and which coincided with my beginning to 'go public' with my psychic experiences and receive coverage in the newspapers and on radio and television.

I dreamed I was in a car among the mountains in some warm, scenic place. There was the sensation of speed. Then the car stopped moving and I saw Princess Rainier – the film star Grace Kelly who had married into the Royal family of Monaco. Grace was being tended by another young lady. After this, the scene changed and I was in a church which was beautifully decorated with lighted candles – but I knew that these were for a funeral service or a memorial.

Three days later we all heard the tragic news that Princess Grace had been travelling, with her daughter in the front passenger seat, on the mountain route between Nice and Monaco when her car had plunged off the road. Neither of them had been wearing seat belts. While her daughter, Stephanie, escaped, Princess Grace died from head injuries. She was fifty-two.

The event was just as I had 'seen' it, and the younger woman tending Princess Grace was her daughter. When we saw the television pictures of the funeral, the array of candles was exactly as I had seen them in the dream – the same colours, light effects and atmosphere.

The entire experience left me feeling overawed and bewildered. I did not know then that this was only among the first of many visions which I was to receive of momentous public events.

4
...

John Lennon, the Pope,
and the Windsor Fire

Sometimes I feel as if I have an early copy of a newspaper in my head. Only this newspaper reports incidents before they happen. 'Visions' for me is a word to be applied quite literally: I don't get vague impressions but powerful pictures. I really see things.

A whole clairvoyance industry has built up over the centuries, and even in Old Testament times King Saul paid a visit to the witch at Endor – and no doubt paid her, too! – in order to discover whether he was destined to win a great battle. Because people, naturally enough, have an interest in what their personal future might hold for them, they are often prepared to part with large sums of money for advance warning and foresight.

I have never taken money for any of my predictions.

I am not saying that all, or even most, clairvoyants are fakes; but the trade does have its share of charlatans. Some of these are extremely clever people in that they are masters (usually mistresses!) of the art of making a little go a very long way – in short, of being vague in their predictions.

Many a fortune teller will say, 'I see a tall, dark stranger', and their client rejoices to see a prediction fulfilled when the man who delivers her new gas-cooker turns out to be a six-foot man with a black beard and a beer-belly! Another favourite among pieces of alleged 'foresight' is: 'You will make a journey over water'. Is this prophecy really fulfilled when I find myself on the boating lake in the park with a couple of grandchildren?

By contrast, my premonitions are usually startlingly precise. For example, on 9 December 1980, I dreamt I saw the ex-Beatle John Lennon walking down a great flight of stairs with a stethoscope around his neck. The scene changed and I was a patient lying in a hospital bed. Lennon came into the room. He was still wearing the stethoscope. I woke up out of the dream very suddenly. John Lennon was in my bedroom, at the bottom of the bed. I knew at once that something dreadful had happened to him.

Next morning I heard the news on the radio and, of course, it was of Lennon's murder outside his New York home by Mark David Chapman. In the days following, the full details of the terrible killing became known and I realised that he had died at more or less the same time as he had appeared in my bedroom.

Why the stethoscope? Why not a gun or an axe? I have no answer, except the suggestion that a stethoscope might indicate a struggle for life, a last desperate attempt to discover life in his body. Alas, it was not to be. My point is only that there was nothing vague about my dream, my premonition: it was entirely plain in the dream aspect and in the later, waking vision when Lennon appeared at the foot of the bed. It was definitely him. There was never any mistaking John Lennon was there? He was distinctive and known worldwide.

There was a custom in the Roman Empire and in other parts of the ancient world that a messenger who brought bad news was put to the sword. Poor chap – it was hardly his fault! Even Jeremiah the prophet was put in a pit for prophesying the fall of Jerusalem. These examples are part of the general suspicion that the bringer of bad news is somehow responsible for the misfortune.

Imagine what havoc this would cause if we applied the principle to television newsreaders: Anna Ford and Trevor MacDonald would hardly last the night! In the same way, witches were tortured and put to death because it was widely believed that they not only predicted what was going to happen, but that their predictions were somehow part of the cause of future events. There is a long tradition of rewarding the harbinger of good tidings and of punishing the prophet of ill-fortune. Think of Joseph in Egypt: in gaol one minute and the next seated at Pharaoh's right hand.

I have absolutely no influence over the content of the messages which I receive. They come to me unbidden and they seem quite fantastic. I certainly do not will the events which appear to me. So what is the relationship between my visions and me? To go back to the example of television: that is just what the visions are like sometimes. You look at the screen and there is a picture, but you have no control over what that picture is. In my visions I don't even have the option of changing channels!

My second sight is also a frequent source of anxiety and distress to me. I don't ask to see vision of catastrophes and disasters – bridges falling, ships sinking and the like. But I have no choice in the matter. I just have to take what comes. So I get to wondering what is the point of tragic premonitions? They cannot be merely random events because they are so precise.

Is it an evil force which causes these visions – as if it were the Devil gloating in advance over evil things which come to pass to destroy people's lives? I don't think so. I believe that all true knowledge comes from God. That is part of the faith which I have tried to keep all my life.

So what is the use of tragic foresight in those cases –

and they are the majority – when I can do nothing to prevent their occurrence? They cannot surely just happen for my entertainment. Indeed, I am not entertained by them but frequently distressed. There have been a few cases in which I have been able to give warning of what I have foreseen and I shall mention some of these incidents in another chapter. But in most cases, I can do nothing to change the future or to avert disaster. So in a world which is good – because God created it – what purpose do such premonitions serve?

Perhaps they are a developing faculty of the human mind: maybe one day we shall all be able to see into the future and doubtless it will be of great value in our planning to avert evil and promote good? Clairvoyance may be an emerging, evolving ability for all humankind and one day we may discover how to use it and to apply it. Be that as it may – and it is only my conjecture – there is nothing I can do with my visions except relate them to you exactly as they happen.

My Catholicism may well be the reason for premonitory visions concerning the Pope. On 9 May 1982, I was getting into bed at about 11pm. As I did so, I began to see the outside of a spectacular castle. It had atmosphere and it was exotic – not just any old place. Out of the castle trooped eight choirboys or, possibly, altar boys.

There were crowds – crowds as in a noisy dream. Thousands of people and confusion on a grand scale. People were running in all directions and calling out anxiously, but no one seemed to know what to do. In the middle of all these people, there was a figure in white – obviously a dignified person, a person of state. I was certain that it was the Pope. Three days later at the shrine of Our Lady of Fatima in Portugal, a man emerged from the seething crowds and tried to stab Pope John Paul II with a bayonet.

The accuracy of this vision is not something which you must take merely on trust from me. The morning after the premonition I recounted it in detail to the parapsychologist Dr Keith Hearne and he made a note of it there and then – three days before the event. 'Three days' is a recurring feature in my predictions; maybe because the number three has been regarded as being of mystical significance by many of the world's great religions and cultures for thousands of years.

There is certainly evidence of a collective consciousness – we see it in all large gatherings whether they are crowds at the sort of religious event presided over by the Pope, or at only football matches. In meetings of this kind, something transcends mere individual consciousness and people seem to feel or sometimes even to speak or shout as one. Perhaps there is also a collective unconscious – as the great psychologist Carl Jung surmised. And maybe this great sum of human experience is a depth into which I reach in my visions. Perhaps, too, this great continuum – conscious/unconscious – can look forward to the future as well as stretch back into the primeval past?

That was not my only premonition concerning the Pope. At exactly 5am on 19 August 1994, I awoke out of a vivid dream. In this dream I was in Rome and looking upwards at the windows in the Vatican. So many tiny windows. Suddenly, at my right hand, the Pope appeared in his outdoor coat which was brilliant white. He too was looking up towards the windows. He seemed to like what he saw because he was smiling a great open smile.

The Vatican windows were convex, polished. In a moment they lost all their brightness and turned dull – as if all the lights had gone out. Next, the Pope appeared at the window and looked down on a great multitude of people who were gathered in the square. It was not the usual crowd of pilgrims from all over the world; they were shouting in anger and threatening voices.

As I awoke out of this dream I was convinced that it was a warning – but a warning about what? Well, there were plans for a Papal visit to Sarajevo and for some reason I knew that my dream had been a caution against his going. I was convinced that he ought not to go there: that there would be an attempt on his life or even, scarcely less dramatic, that the visit might test his health beyond what he could endure.

In fact, the Pope cancelled his visit to Sarajevo on the grounds that his security could not be guaranteed; and because there was widespread opposition and danger threatened by some of the parties to the strife in Bosnia. At the time of the cancellation of the planned visit, one of the Pope's doctors said that he was 'psychologically unwell' and that he was suffering from 'great mental anguish'. This anguish or anxiety had been a very power-ful aspect of my dream on 19 August. Dr Corrado Mani said, 'The Pope suffers private agonies because he wants to do so much but his aging body will not let him.' This was exactly the feeling of frustration and anxiety which permeated my dream.

I mentioned 'three days' as a kind of motif which features in many of my premonitions. 'Three weeks' is a similar pattern. Three weeks after my 5am dream about the Pope, there were newspaper reports about a health scare regarding him. In fact there were rumours to the effect that he had died. These rumours were sparked off when an elderly Polish Cardinal was seen running through the Vatican gates at 5am on Sunday 11 September – just three weeks after my dream.

I had clearly picked up in my psychic dream the flavour of the great cloud of free-floating anxiety surrounding the health and welfare of the Pope. People were anxious about him, and that anxiety was focused on the appearance of a particular Cardinal at exactly the hour of day at which my dream had happened three weeks beforehand.

Psychic experiences are feelings, sensations. What I had unconsciously tuned into were the collective anxieties of people close to the Pope. Naturally I am glad that he did not go to Sarajevo and get shot by a sniper; and I am delighted that he did not die at home in the Vatican from natural causes. But the fact that neither of these things occurred does not mean that my premonition failed. I had never claimed that the Pope would get shot or that he would die in his bed at that time. But events confirmed that there was widespread anxiety about those two matters at exactly the time envisaged in my dream.

Enormous numbers of people feel attachment to prominent people such as the Pope and John Lennon. In an age of mass communications, this is one factor which leaders and notables from different areas of life have in common. The Pope and the pop star share a similar sort of adulation. I believe that it is this great surge of collective feeling which somehow impinges on my own sensitivities and gets translated into visionary experiences.

Huge outpourings of collective emotion – wishes, hopes fears or prayers – sometimes overspill, as it were, into physical events in the material world. For example, it was widely claimed that the corporate prayers of the whole nation produced the calm seas and the mild weather which enabled the Dunkirk evacuations in 1940.

Nationhood and national symbols might reasonably be supposed to produce similar powerful emotions. The Royal Family, for example, and particularly the Monarch, are almost like magical or mythological personages. A great deal of collective emotion attaches to them. Crowds turn out to see them. Even at this late date in the twentieth century, royalty and royal things evoke awe and wonder bordering on religious devotion. Just recall how many visitors turn out every year to see the Crown Jewels or the royal palaces.

It is a particular royal palace which features in one of my recent visions. On 17 November 1992, I dreamt about the Queen Mother. She was standing, distraught, her hands clasped in front of her, while behind her a great palace was ablaze. I could not make out which of the royal palaces this might be, but three days later, there occurred the disastrous fire at Windsor Castle. There is no doubt in my mind that this dream was a direct foreseeing of the catastrophe.

Why the Queen Mother? Why should she feature in the premonition? I did a little research after the event and I learned that, along with Sandringham, Windsor is one of the Queen Mother's favourite homes. This is interesting to me in itself. I didn't know before the dream and before the fire how she felt about Windsor. So my unconscious, dreaming mind obviously knew something which my consciousness did not know. Where could this knowledge have originated except from that corporate pool or reservoir of knowledge and experience which is referred to as the collective unconscious?

This is not a fanciful, new notion. The Bible and the Church teach that, although we usually experience time and place in little segments which we call 'the here and now', we are really part of something infinitely greater and more interesting. The Bible refers to this greater personal reality as 'The Whole Company of Heaven' and the Church speaks of 'The Communion of Saints'.

The traditional Catholic faith teaches us that we are not alone in our little time and locale, but that we are 'compassed about by a great cloud of witnesses'. I believe this. I know that this is true. And my knowledge is not theoretical. I know it to be true from my personal, undeniable experience which has been proved again and again over a lifetime of visionary experiences which must come from somewhere. I have no doubt but that they are aspects of this great spiritual continuum of past, present and future. We know that time is only relative. It is only one dimension. We know that the past is never entirely dead and buried – that the events of the past shape the present and that people and places from what has gone by live on in the memory.

I have no doubt that the future also can appear in the present. I know this because it has actually happened to me – not once but hundreds of times. What is 'the present' anyway? It is, in my view, only a small part – a snapshot, if you like – of the whole of eternity. We cannot move events about physically in the vast continuum of time, but these events do seem to move about mentally or spiritually in time. And I believe that my visions and premonitions are aspects of these movements. They seem to occur not for trivial events but when a great deal of human emotion – joy or pain – is attached to them.

This is a great comfort in a way, even when what I foresee turns out to be a catastrophe. For it seems to demonstrate that the feelings we have about the world are part of the fabric of the world itself, that our hopes and fears are aspects of an eternal pattern of which my visions are only a small part.

5
...

Death on the High Seas and a Miracle at Home

Roland and I were beginning to experience the joys and the expense of a growing family and so I began to look around for a part-time job which would bring in a few pounds each week. There was a job advertised – housework – at a big house in Beverley Road, Kirkella, which was the part of Hull I had always regarded as 'posh'. I went along one day to apply for it.

Well, I was overawed. Posh it certainly was. It was the home of Mr and Mrs Shannon. Their son was the chairman of a leading electrical retail conglomerate and the house was elegantly tasteful with large, exquisitely decorated rooms. Mrs Shannon was my idea of a real lady. I was nervous under all those high ceilings, but to my surprise I was offered the job immediately. I worked there on weekday mornings for eight years and I can truthfully say that I was welcomed as a member of the family. At ten minutes before midday – the hour when I finished work – the Shannons always called me into the morning room for a glass of sherry.

My nervousness at finding myself in such grand company spilled over into what I suppose we should call a domestic psychic experience. I can laugh at it now, but at the time I was shaking with apprehension. Mrs Shannon owned some beautiful crystal lamps which I used to polish with a carefulness bordering on trepidation. One night I dreamt I had broken off three of these crystals while cleaning them and I awoke in a panic. Three weeks later, my dream came true. I remember saying aloud to myself, 'I wish I didn't work here!' – I was so apprehensive.

Anxiously, I went to Mrs Shannon to tell her what had happened. I was in tears. Mrs Shannon was the director of a nursing home and she was about to set off for her regular meeting. When she saw that I was crying, she said, 'Whatever is the matter?' I could hardly bring myself to tell her. When I had told her, she said, 'Dear Barbara, don't be upset! Those crystals can be easily replaced.'

I tell this story partly to reveal how nervous I was working at the grand house, but also to explain something about my psychic gift. It can seem like a curse rather than a blessing sometimes: for I had no power to stop my dream about the broken crystals from coming true. Sometimes people think that because I am psychic I can control the future. Well I can't. I merely see things which turn out to be inevitable; but I can do nothing myself to avert events – be they appalling tragedies like plane crashes or trivial mishaps like Mrs Shannon's broken – and easily repairable! – crystals.

There was one huge psychic event which concerned the Shannons. Every winter, just before Christmas, they used to sail for Cape Town and the sunshine. In November 1981, Mrs Shannon had suffered a bout of pneumonia and she was looking forward to the trip even more than usual because it would give her the chance to convalesce. Mr Shannon gave me the house keys and all my instructions over a glass of sherry as usual. He was a fine, kind and elegant man – certainly what might be called 'officer class'. In fact he had served as a Group Captain in the New Zealand Air Force, and he would still put on his uniform for ceremonial occasions.

Three weeks before they were due to sail, I dreamt I was on the seashore and I began to float out to sea – not on the surface of the water, but as if drifting through the air about it. I floated like this right out to sea and there I saw a beautiful ocean liner, but I could not make out its name. Later I realised that this was because the ship's name was written in Greek: ΑΧΙΛΛΕ ΛΑΥΡΟ – *The Achille Lauro*.

There, right out at sea, I saw three coffins come up the gangway and I wondered why this should be happening while the ship was not docked. Behind the coffins were flames. I agonised over whether to tell Mrs Shannon what I had dreamed. I discussed the dream with Roland, but still I hesitated. Desperately, I wanted to say, 'Please don't go on the voyage!' But what would they make of my warning? Wouldn't they just think I was raving?

On the day of their departure I watched their car go down the drive and I wanted above all to call them back – but still I held back. I said aloud, 'If anything happens to them, I'll never be able to forgive myself!'

They set sail. After a few days, her daughter Barbara phoned me and said 'Mum's OK.'

I said, 'Yes, I know – she's over the pneumonia nicely.'

'No, not that. There's been a fire on *The Achille Lauro* and two people have died. They were taken off in mid-ocean.'

I could hardly breathe with the shock of the news. I heard myself saying, 'Yes, but were there only two?' It must have sounded a very perplexing thing to say in the circumstances; but then Barbara replied, 'Two people died, but then another passenger was so distraught when he learned of his wife's death that he threw himself over the side. That makes three deaths in all.'

Eventually, Mrs Shannon returned, but I never said a word to her about these things.

Around this time, Dr Keith Hearne, a psychologist with a special interest in the paranormal advertised in the *Hull Daily Mail* for people who had received premonitions to get in touch with him for the purposes of his research. I didn't see the advert, but my sister Phyllis wrote to Dr Hearne on my behalf.

He phoned and I met him and completed some psychometric tests and a questionnaire. Later he asked me to a meeting at the Station Hotel in Hull with other local psychic ladies. A reporter from the *Sunday Mirror* was there as well. After this, Dr Hearne sent me a supply of stamped addressed envelopes and I filled them in with my premonitions for a whole year. Many of these came true. In fact, Dr Hearne said I had a very good striking rate – something like eighty per cent.

At the end of January 1982, I dreamt I was on board a ship and that I was talking to Roland's mother. I was saying to her, 'The water is like a boiling cauldron.' I woke up saying, 'The Diddymen!' which must have sounded barmy even to Roland who was used to my strange dreams by now! I notified this premonition to Dr Hearne.

Three weeks later, a ship, *The Victory* sank. It was an oil tanker which had come to grief leaving the port of Liverpool – my dream reference to the Diddymen (the fictional creation of Liverpudlian comedian Ken Dodd). The newspaper reported the words of one of the crew, a survivor, saying, 'The water was like a cauldron.' The *Sunday Mirror* ran the story of my prediction on the front page!

On 15 April 1982, I was watching the BBC lunchtime programme Pebble Mill At One. Arthur Lowe, the actor who played Captain Mainwaring in the long-running favourite show *Dad's Army*, was being interviewed. Suddenly, his chair seemed to be empty, then his image returned. I called Roland and asked if he thought Arthur Lowe looked ill. 'No. He looks perfectly well to me,' said Roland.

But I was overwhelmed with the sad impression that he would die soon, and I said so. That night we were having drinks with Roland's brother and my sister-in-law, Laura, when the late night news came on television. Arthur Lowe had died.

Another of my premonitions validated by Dr Hearne around this time concerned the actor Lionel Jeffries. I dreamed he was in a boat, rowing, and that he had a narrow escape. This came true exactly three weeks later.

People refer to my psychic gift as if it is part of some huge glamorous lifestyle. But my ordinary domestic life has always carried on its same daily routine despite the strange and powerful visions and intimations of things to come. I must repeat therefore that I regard myself as an ordinary person just like my neighbours and everyone else: the only difference being that I am an ordinary person to whom the most extraordinary things seem to happen from time to time.

And ordinary people suffer their ordinary difficulties and trials. I have recounted some of these personal troubles already; but there were more and greater trials to come.

In 1975, when he was only forty-five, Roland suffered a whole series of strokes. I put it all down to his earlier attack of meningitis. Whatever the cause, my husband became very seriously ill – just how ill I discovered only much later.

He had been to a friend's house. He came home and dropped his knife during the evening meal. His mouth seemed to sag on one side and he could barely speak. I phoned the doctor. A neurosurgeon, Dr Rawson, attended Roland and diagnosed a slight stroke. Roland has his stubborn side and refused to go into hospital. I knew that he had a fear of our not being able to manage financially if he ever became ill, so he was putting on a tremendously brave face.

In 1978, he was winding the clock when he developed similar symptoms to those he had suffered before. This time Dr Rawson insisted that he go into hospital – a decision which may well have saved Roland's life, for he had another stroke on the following day and yet another the day after that.

He stayed in hospital for a week and recovered his speech and movement, came home and insisted he was going back to work at the Blackburn aircraft factory. He got up early in the morning but he collapsed downstairs while he was making the tea. I ran down and lifted him on to a chair – God only knows where I drew the strength from to move him! The emergency doctor came at nine o'clock.

Again Roland seemed to make a full recovery and, after a fortnight, he did go back to work. This is where a psychic experience burst into our mundane problems. I was on the bus with our son John who was then aged about eight. Suddenly I saw a vision of an ambulance outside our door. And when we arrived home there was an ambulance. They had brought Roland home from work. Again it was a stroke.

The next day Roland tripped on the landing at home but he insisted he was all right. We had an appointment for him at the surgery which was full. As we were sitting there, I noticed that a man opposite was staring at my husband. He had suffered yet another stroke, there in the doctor's waiting-room! This must have been about his sixth.

This time he did go into hospital for tests. One evening when I was visiting, the neurosurgeon – not Dr Rawson – was there as well. He noticed Roland's tobacco pouch on the counterpane and he said, 'You might just as well go ahead and smoke as much as you like; but if you do you'll have a massive stroke tonight and you'll end up like a cabbage!'

Roland never smoked again.

At last the cause of the trouble was diagnosed. The arteries in Roland's neck had deteriorated so far as to have almost disintegrated. He was referred to one of the country's top neurosurgeons, Mrs Bannister. She had very short straight hair and a stoop and was very unprepossessing to look at, yet I have no hesitation in saying that she was the most beautiful person I have ever met. I can see that extra personal dimension, the psychic aura which is the signature of the personality or, as used to be said, the soul. She was a wonderful person.

Mrs Bannister was based at Crumpsall Hospital in Manchester and Roland went there for further tests. In the evening after the tests had been completed, Mrs Bannister herself phoned me from the hospital to tell me she would operate on Roland the very next day. It was his only chance.

I had promised Roland (and myself) that, if he required an operation, I would be there to see him come round from the anaesthetic. But how could I get to Manchester at such short notice? We were flat broke and in any case I don't drive. Our daughter Linda had just had her third baby. She came to see me and she said she would book me into a guest house in Manchester. In truth, I didn't have a clue where I was going to raise the money to pay for the stay.

That evening there was a knock at the door. It was Geoff, one of Roland's workmates, and he said, 'We've had a whipround and the lads have collected a hundred and fifty quid for Roland. It's the biggest collection we've ever had.' And there was the money in a plastic wallet –

coins and notes all together, just as it had been collected from the men. I burst into tears. I didn't want others to pay for me, but what could I do? That gift strengthened my faith enormously and it seemed to augur that Roland would get well. But it was still touch and go.

I was to be driven to Crumpsall by Sandra's husband. On the morning of Roland's operation at about ten o'clock, just the hour when Roland was going into the operating theatre, I saw a vision of a great white whirl-wind in our front room. I said aloud, 'I know you're going to be all right, darling!' I believe in the depths of my being that that whirlwind was the Holy Spirit – a sign to me that Roland would recover. But we weren't out of the wood yet.

On the motorway we had a burst tyre and the car careered across the road, quite out of control. I don't know how my son-in-law retrieved the situation, for it seemed without doubt we would be killed. But we were guided – that's just what it felt like, as if unseen hands had seized the car to right it – back to the left side of the road and we proceeded on our way.

At the hospital in Crumpsall there is a corridor half a mile long and, as we walked down it, it seemed twice that distance. Along that corridor we met Mrs Bannister on her way from the operation. She said, 'Hello there, Barbara! Roland will be pleased to see you.'

There are no words for the joyful turbulence I felt at the moment Mrs Bannister added, 'I think I've given him a few more years.'

When I went into the ward and saw Roland, he looked like the Elephant Man. He had fifty stitches in his wound, but in eight days they had all been removed and Roland was home. Mrs Bannister had performed miracles – even achieving a bypass of troublesome arteries in Roland's brain itself.

He has suffered 'little epilepsies' since, but nothing compared with the life-threatening strokes of the earlier years. Later, I asked Mrs Bannister how long Roland would have lived if she had not operated.

She replied, 'I would have given him three weeks.'

As I sit here writing these words, I reckon on my fingers: she has given him fourteen years ... and counting.

6

...

Fire, Assassination and Murder Most Foul

There are so many ways in which psychic ability shows itself. If someone gives me an object, I can frequently tell them something about themselves. This is called psychometry, which I will say more about later. For example, when I had been helping to make a television programme about psychic experiences, the producer handed me his watch. I immediately had a strong sense that he lived near some railway sidings. He did. There was also a feeling that nearby was some sort of private hospital or nursing home. There was.

I sensed that there would be an accident resulting in a fire at the nursing home. Some little time later, the producer phoned me to say that there had indeed been a fire there.

There was another classic 'three weeks' premonition around this time. I dreamt I was in the Seychelles – strange how I get these indubitable feelings for place: I have never been to the Seychelles! I was on a cliff edge and I saw a figure by my side. Three weeks later, it was announced that a member of the cast of the television soap opera *Crossroads* had disappeared in the Seychelles.

Sport was once the subject of a sad predictive dream of mine. I saw a boxing ring and one of the boxers, trying to get into the ring, dropped down dead. This happened the very next night when Phil Crates, a Hull boxer, died in exactly this way. On the brighter side: I am quite a connoisseur of football and I can boast that I have predicted the winners of thirty-eight out of forty Cup Finals!

A number of times, as I was getting into bed, I seemed to be presented with a television set in part of a waking vision. In the Old Testament, Daniel saw the writing on the wall, but I see the pictures on the TV! Perhaps even something so ancient as psychic awareness changes its style in keeping with advances in technology?

In April 1982, I was on my way to bed when on the imagined television screen I saw an amphibious craft. There were also aircraft-carriers, larger ships and aeroplanes. I saw foreign words on the screen – as I had done earlier in the case of the *Achille Lauro* – and I couldn't make out their meaning. Three nights later there came news of the surprise Argentinean attack on the Falkland Islands. The planes and the amphibious craft which we saw on the television news that night were the same as those I had seen in my waking vision.

Also in 1982, I dreamt I was standing in a courtyard in front of a palace with railings which looked rather drab. I recognised it – partly by the drabness, I have to admit! – as Buckingham Palace. There was a single light high up in a solitary window. At the time I sensed that the light itself referred to the Queen, and I suspected that she was in some danger – though I also surmised that the very brightness of the light was a sign that Her Majesty would not come to serious harm.

This all happened at the time when I had begun to send my dreams and premonitions to Dr Keith Hearne. I told him of this one. My premonition was taken up by Alan Bestock of *Woman's Own* magazine and, as I learned later, the palace were informed and they put on extra security. Even so, an intruder did manage to gain unauthorised access to Buckingham Palace that year: Michael Fagan managed to reach the Queen's bedchamber, sit on the edge of her bed and smoke a cigarette.

Concerning Dr Hearne himself, I had a dream which nonplussed us both at the time. I dreamt he was in the Royal Albert Hall. He was wearing a red jacket and matching bow tie, and holding a baton. Now whatever is a psychologist doing dressed as a conductor? However, years later Keith wrote a Requiem Mass which was published. We had not, up to the time of my dream even so much as chatted about music.

Sometimes a premonition is so loaded with sadness and anguish that to receive it is a terrible burden. One such premonition came to me in 1983. I remember it precisely for the reason that it came to take up so much of my time and cause me a great deal of heartache.

It was 3.15 Friday afternoon and Roland and I were on our way to collect John from school in the car. We were waiting for a set of traffic lights to change when I heard the phrase 'Boy murdered!' It came to me just like that: tersely and without any warning – like the shrill cry of a newsvendor on a street corner. That's all that was said, but I was instantly filled with apprehension.

I knew somehow that the murder had taken place quite near to where I had heard its announcement. Three weeks later it was announced that a boy's body had been found wrapped in plastic in a nearby park. This park is along one of the roads where we sat waiting for the traffic lights to change.

One night just after this, I was sitting in the bath when I saw a vision of a set of yellow oilskins – the sort worn by fishermen. I also saw the name 'Sue Ryder'. Years later the murdered boy's father died in a Sue Ryder hospital. I also dreamt I saw three men in motorcycle wear and that there was an element of sexual perversion involved. I told all these things to the police who were economical with what they actually told me in return; but they did say that my information had helped them a lot.

For one thing, though the murderers were never caught, the police told me that their strongest indications pointed to the culprits being a gang of sexual perverts.

I was so moved by these sad events that I determined to do all I could to help the police. I tried to reconstruct the murder in the light of the various visions and intuitions I had received about it. Roland drove me to the area where Christopher had lived. There I sensed strongly that the murder had actually taken place between two embankments. We took a few wrong turnings and almost got ourselves lost. Roland stopped the car. There we were – between two high embankments.

I got out of the car and began to snoop around, hardly knowing what I was looking for. I just sensed that this was the place where the awful events had occurred. Suddenly, I came upon an old bridge which trawlermen used to cross over the lock. Then I understood that the yellow oilskins were showing me trawlermen. I was as certain as I have ever been of anything that this was the very location of the murder.

The stream ran down from the lock until it became the beck where the police had found the boy's body. My conjecture, supported by all my instincts and premonitory sense, was that here indeed the lad had met his cruel death at the hands of a band of sexual perverts, and that his body, placed in the plastic covering, had floated down to the part of the stream known as Beverley Beck.

This episode filled me with a sense of unease which has never entirely gone away. I felt so strongly – and I still feel – that I saw in my inner space what had befallen poor young Christopher. I saw it so clearly, it was like watching a film. Yet I could do nothing more to help bring his killers to justice. To have knowledge and yet to remain impotent, as I was in this case, is a heavy burden to bear.

People often say they envy me my psychic gift. But would they, really, in a case like this where an innocent boy was slain and I, seeing the terrible details, was powerless to help?

The first time I came across psychometry, which I mentioned briefly at the beginning of this chapter, was when a lady rang me after one of my appearances on Radio Humberside and asked if I 'did psychometry'. In those days, I didn't even know the meaning of the word! But in due course I was able to tell her things about her husband's business; and on one occasion I told her the surname of the gynaecologist who was treating her daughter in the Cayman Islands!

The psychic gift does not make me cleverer than other people. It is a diffuse and shimmering gift, and I am not always the best person to interpret the dreams or voices. I am always ready and willing for anyone to help me with a particular interpretation.

When I say diffuse, I mean that although there have been many startlingly exact and vivid predictions, the psychic sense is often more subtle than that – less dramatic, if you like, but very real nonetheless. One of the ways in which my psychic awareness shows itself is in my ability to know what is in the mind of a person whom I have only just met. And not only that, but I seem to know the character of the person, what he is like inwardly. I have even given character readings and appraisals based on this kind of insight.

When I review my life, I feel that I have been extraordinarily happy and uncommonly blessed; but I am bound also to reflect that we have endured a great deal of sadness through bereavement and illness. There is a tradition that those who inherit spiritual gifts pay the price in personal suffering. I mention this only because it seems to have been true in the lives of so many psychics from Saint Paul (with his 'thorn in the flesh') to the more ordinary clairvoyants of our own age. Of course, I wouldn't have anyone say that I was some sort of martyr: on the contrary, I am a naturally cheerful and optimistic person and above all I have strong faith in God and in his good purposes. If I have been sent sufferings, then I have also been given the strength, through love, to come through them.

The prophet is frequently disturbed and even horrified by the destruction and carnage which he or she foresees. I have often asked myself why it is that so many of my premonitions – and indeed those of most clairvoyants – feature disaster. Perhaps there is an answer to this question, but first let me tell you of one of my most striking visions.

In September 1981, I was asleep and dreaming of a warm country and I knew in the dream that there was sand in the place. I was in a stadium where I saw military men with coffee-coloured faces. They were wearing olive-green uniforms. In front of these men was a row of dignitaries in dark suits which may have been formal dress or else some sort of uniform. Suddenly, the men in olive uniforms ran forward and poured bullets into the chief of the dignitaries.

Three weeks later, precisely, on 6 October 1981, President Sadat of Egypt was assassinated by members of his bodyguard as he reviewed his troops at a ceremony to commemorate the anniversary of the Yom Kippur war. The dress and style of his assassins – coffee-coloured faces and olive-green uniforms – was exactly as in my dream.

Now why should I foresee such a terrible event and not, say, a forthcoming tea party or a charity ball? I think it is because the psychic sense, like any other sense, tunes itself to the strongest signals, like a radio set. And the strongest signals are naturally those surrounded by powerful emotions. This has always been the case from the prophecies we find in the Bible to the premonitions of contemporary clairvoyants. The great psychologist Jung said that powerful emotions generate psychic energy; and I believe that it is this energy which psychics tune in to.

It's not that psychics are morbid creatures who always look on the black side – anyone who knows me would say just the opposite! But tragedy and disaster cause great turmoil and upheaval in the psychic dimension, and so it is only to be expected that a sensitive person would pick up these disturbances. Bad news always seems to generate more interest than good news. You only have to open a newspaper or look at the news on television: usually, the announcer might just as well begin with, 'And here's Trevor bringing you news of fresh disasters!'

Sometimes a premonition concerns not some great global event but a domestic or personal matter very near to the heart of the clairvoyant. I have already mentioned a few such visions and premonitions about members of my own family. Another particularly strong one of these happened in the same year that I foresaw the assassination of President Sadat.

My son Paul was twenty in 1981 and he was very much in love with his girlfriend, Annetta, who had been his sweetheart from the age of sixteen. I knew that they planned to set up home together before marrying. I'm old fashioned to a degree, I suppose; but I did not disapprove of their planned arrangement – I just did not expect that it would happen so soon!

One day a letter arrived for Paul and I just knew that it would be about a house they would share. I wanted him to be happy, but I simply dreaded his leaving home. I was clinging, even though I tried not to show it.

That day Roland and I were entertaining friends. I just had to get out of the house, though, and asked if they would mind if I went for a walk. This was, I know, extremely rude of me, and it was something I would never usually contemplate. But this day was different, and I did. I knew that Paul would be coming home, and I just had to be out of the house when he arrived.

While I was gone, Paul came home and went out again. It was, as I had guessed, the day when he would make his move to leave home and set up with Annetta. I can't remember where I wandered to while I was out, but when I returned Roland told me I had been gone for four hours. My time alone, wandering around the town, had helped me come to terms with Paul's departure. I also went, as soon as I could, to Mass and thanked God that Paul was so happy. The walk and the Mass, taken together, were like some exorcism of my worries and bad feelings. Paul and Annetta have long since married and of course Roland and I are on excellent terms with them.

The Wilberforce House Museum in Hull is dedicated to the memory of William Wilberforce, the great nineteenth-century parliamentarian and anti-slaver. In the middle of one night in 1982 I heard the words, 'Wilberforce House broken into!' Shortly after this dream, Robin Pulford was hosting a programme about clairvoyance on Radio Humberside. I phoned in and told him of what I had dreamt in detail: that the museum would be broken into from two doors away and that a quantity of silver would be stolen.

Roland and I went on holiday, and the museum was robbed while we were away. Now the strange thing about this particular premonition is that I had had my dream months before the event; but the actual break-in occurred exactly three weeks after I had made the contents of the dream known to Robin Pulford on his show. Three weeks, or three days – this time interval is a common feature in so many of my premonitions.

After Roland's brain operation he really needed to convalesce. In fact, I would have said there was a strong case for his taking invalidity retirement. But you just try telling Roland that! He wanted to work. He is a proud man, and he desired above all to provide for his family. I don't know how he struggled in to work some of the mornings; and in the evenings our son would go to meet him and help him from the bus to the front door.

We decided that we needed a bungalow since the stairs were becoming increasingly difficult for Roland. There was a suitable place in Hathersedge Road and we went to view it. The owner was called Peter, a nice man – so much so that, when I met him, I heard a voice inside my head saying, 'This shouldn't happen to you – you're so nice!'

There was a long delay in the purchase proceedings occasioned, as I later discovered, by the fact that Peter was in the throes of a marital separation. At first I thought that had been what the voice referred to. Then one night I dreamt I was in a sort of arena and Peter was there. He was saying, 'Didn't you know – I've got cancer?'

The next day I phoned Peter's mother and she confirmed that he did in fact have cancer. He was given a bone marrow transplant and I think he made a complete recovery.

7

...

The Dingo Baby Trial,
Indira Gandhi and Terry Waite

The 1980s were the years when my psychic gift flourished and the premonitions came thick and fast. It did not seem strange to me any more: of course, I was always amazed by the frequency and the accuracy of the predictions, but I came to see the dreams and visions as belonging to me, as part of my personality. I suppose I am trying to say that from this time onwards I did not regard the occurrence of the visions as some kind of intrusion. I was learning fully to accept my gift.

It also became clear to me that psychic ability runs in the family to a much greater extent than I had thought. I have explained that my father was psychic; in 1982 I had to accept that my son Jon had inherited something of the gift as well.

He went on a school skiing holiday in Bulgaria. Not long after he had returned home, he dreamt that the hotel where he had stayed caught fire and that two boys died in the blaze. This came true shortly afterwards, and naturally enough Jon was greatly disturbed, not only by the tragedy itself in which lads of his own age had perished, but also by the fact that, in his dream, he had foreseen it all. I comforted him by explaining that the fire was not his fault, and that visions of things to come arrive unbidden and unsought. I knew what agonies these experiences can cause, and I did not want my son, at his tender age –

he was twelve at the time – to become bowed down with guilt and confusion over events that were in no way his doing.

Meanwhile, Roland, having made a good recovery from the brain surgery, began to suffer a series of mild heart attacks. These worsened, but Roland – with his customary determination – would hear nothing of going into hospital for a spell.

One day in 1983, we met a man called Len Hazel who worked for the Samaritans. Len was the very essence of kindness. One of his clients, Christine, was greatly helped by Len's gentleness and encouragement and she and her husband – knowing that Len was 74 and that he lived on his own – asked him if he would like to move in with them. The arrangement was mutually beneficial. The couple thought the world of the old man.

One day, when Christine and her husband were on holiday, we invited Len round for tea. I had heard from Christine that he had healing gifts, and so, given my increasing concern for Roland, I asked Len if he would administer the Laying on of Hands. Len put his hands on Roland's head and said straight away, 'Changing religion!' And it was true – though Len would not have known it: for Roland had spoken to no one but myself of his desire to embrace my faith and become a Roman Catholic.

While Len was placing his hands on Roland's head, I seemed to hear, inwardly, two words: 'superficial injuries'. I had no idea at the time what these words might signify; but I wrote them down on a piece of paper.

Suddenly, I developed an irritating numbness in my cheek and I asked Len to place his hands on me too. As he did so, I had a vivid impression of two or three sets of traffic lights. These seemed to be connected with Len. I asked him if he regularly went near sets of lights such as

I had envisioned and he said there were some quite near to where he was living, and that he was obliged to negotiate them every day.

I warned him to take extra care. We changed the subject after this, and began to talk about holidays. It turned out that Len knew a place which Roland and I were very fond of: Cockington in Devon. Len said he had a souvenir of the place – a little brass pixie – and that he would give it to me.

A few days later, Len was knocked down at a set of traffic lights near his home. We were devastated. I asked the policeman how badly hurt he was, and the policeman said, 'Not badly: only superficial injuries.' Superficial injuries – the very words I had heard inwardly as Len had lain his hands on my head! The original injuries had indeed been only minor, but there were complications, and Len died that night from a blood clot in the brain.

After poor, kind old Len's funeral, I told Christine about the Cockington pixie and she looked for it throughout the house – without luck. At last she found it, in Len's overcoat pocket. He had been bringing it to me, as he had promised, on the day he died.

As I mentioned earlier, I had many premonitions in the 1980s. I have tried to describe how some of these predictions are quite literal, explicit and exact while others are more like hints – symbolic images which are difficult to understand and interpret at the time but which become clear as events unfold. At the beginning of March 1981 I received a premonition which combined symbol with reality, fact with fiction.

I dreamt I was in the back seat of a black limousine. Driving the car was the famous actor, Trevor Howard. I knew it was Howard because I had seen him many times in films and also I recognised him, as he turned his head, from the slight pockmarking on his face. His front-seat passenger was a sinister man with a Swastika armband.

We stopped and another limousine crossed our path. There was another famous actor in this car too, but I could not make out his face precisely. Both cars came to a halt, whereupon the man with the Swastika armband got out of our car and the film star got out of his. The SS man shot the actor and I heard the wail of sirens, the screams of the crowds and all the pandemonium of crisis.

Exactly three weeks later, on 30 March, President Ronald Reagan was shot by John Hinkley – a man who was revealed to have been a member of an American neo-Nazi group. Why did Trevor Howard feature in the dream? This bit of symbolism was not at all difficult for me to interpret – after the event! Howard and Reagan had played similar roles in Hollywood movies.

I was beginning to understand how literal representation and symbolic images combine in the visionary experience. One of my first inklings of this combination had in fact happened some time before the assassination attempt on President Reagan. In 1980, I dreamt I was in Australia.

I was walking on my own and I saw some impressive buildings in a crescent. I understood them to be a law court. There was a woman walking by herself and, some way behind her – as if he had something to do with her but was trying to distance himself – there followed a man. I heard the words, 'Dingo, Alice Springs'. At that time no news had been broadcast of the notorious murder case in which a mother alleged that it was not she but a wild dog that had killed her child. At the trial she was convicted of the killing and her husband – who I took to be the man who followed at a distance in my dream – was acquitted.

My most strikingly symbolic premonition bordered on the surreal – something of which Salvador Dali himself would have been proud. It was 1983 and I saw a vision of

Mrs Thatcher in a brightly-coloured sari with a costume jacket over the top. And you can't get much more bizarre than that! It was not, however, a light-hearted or entertaining vision; for this strange figure was shot without warning by some men who surrounded her.

This was a year before the assassination of Mrs Gandhi. The sari was symbolic of her, personally; and the face of Mrs Thatcher was what indicated her rank to me as a national leader. Bizarre, if you like, but in retrospect, the meaning is obvious. Perhaps it ought to have been obvious at the time. But I have already explained that I am not always expert in the interpretation of what is given to me. Vision and interpretation are often two quite different phenomena. I take some comfort from the fact that, as recorded in his letter to the Corinthians, Saint Paul thought the same. He said that there were those who spoke in tongues, and then there were in addition those who interpreted what was being said.

Len's intuition that Roland would change his religion came true in 1985 when my husband asked Father Ryan for instruction into the Catholic faith. We went along to the presbytery every Friday, and my abiding memory is of how ill Roland looked. He still suffered the small heart attacks but I felt that, whatever he suffered, he would recover: for each time he had one of his attacks, I saw hands outstretched above him to heal and console. But I also always saw Roland's white duvet in the colour of operation-theatre green.

One Friday, Roland was too ill to go to class – so ill in fact that he was admitted into Castle Hill hospital to prepare for an angiogram examination. The consultant, Mr Nair, was severe in his manner of speech, and this upset us. He was a brilliant surgeon and the brusqueness was just his style; but to say he had no bedside manner would be to put it mildly!

The angiogram revealed that Roland was so ill that he must not be allowed to go home to await surgery, but that he would have to be operated on almost immediately if he was to have any chance of survival, let alone recovery. The ward sister told me that he was so poorly that he mustn't even lift a teacup.

Mr Nair's deputy asked to see the whole family and he explained to us that Roland would have to endure four heart bypasses. It was an intensely emotional time in all our lives. I phoned Father Ryan and said, 'When it comes to the designation at the bottom of his bed, what is Roland's religion?' He said, 'Roland is a Catholic.'

Next morning, the day of the operation, all the family including our five grandchildren went to Mass. As I knelt at the altar rail, my crucifix and necklace fell into my outstretched hand, intact. How could that have come about? There were no loose or broken links on the chain. I took it to be reassurance that Roland would recover. He did. But that year, 1985, was the longest year of our lives.

Roland suffered a great deal, so much so that he would break down in anguish and say that, if he had known what he would have to go through, he would never have agreed to the heart surgery. He asked me why he had not died. Why had he been spared? I said, 'You have been through all these traumas, darling, but you have life. That is the greatest gift. God has given us this life together. God loves you.'

That night when we were in bed, I was drifting off to sleep when I heard myself say to Roland, 'There – I told you so!'

Only later did Roland tell me that he had been in agony of mind and spirit and he had asked God why he had been spared. God's voice had come to him saying, 'Because I love you'. This was the point at which I had said, 'There – I told you so!' But how? I had not heard the voice inside Roland's head, but I had made the appropriate response right on cue.

He did begin to recover and we thought we might make things easier for him if we moved to a new bungalow. There was a pretty little place which we had our eyes on in Aldborough, a village about fifteen miles up the coast towards Bridlington. This was the occasion for another demonstration of our son Jon's psychic abilities. Before we had expressed any intention of moving, he said one night, 'We're going to leave this house. I know, because when I look at the walls in the living room they're all bare.' And so they became.

In the new bungalow, Jon, who was about twelve at the time, said he heard the bathroom cistern flush some twenty minutes after any of us had vacated the loo! A small incident, but one which added to my belief that he had inherited the psychic ability. Soon after this episode he told me that, as he was recovering from a migraine headache, he saw very close to him the face of a young girl. Her function seemed to be to lead him out of the migraine, though at the time he was more terrified than comforted. From what he told me, I became sure that it was his sister Angela who had died in infancy all those years ago.

I loved the bungalow in Aldborough. We had an open fire and the general atmosphere was so peaceful. I used to clean out the grate every morning. One day while I was doing this, I heard the word 'Svengali!' I had no idea what it meant. I asked Roland and he told me that Svengali is a magician and stage performer.

I said, 'A trick – and it will go wrong.' Soon after there came news of a magician called Svengali whose best-known trick involved his pretending to catch in his teeth a bullet fired at him by someone in the audience. Of course, it was only a trick – the bullet was always a blank. But at one fateful performance, the member of the audience chosen to shoot the gun fired a real bullet at the magician. Svengali was shot dead.

1987 was the year when – quite unexpectedly to me! – I began my writing career. I wanted to do something to express my thanks to Mrs Bannister who had performed brain surgery on Roland all those years before. I knew that she was engaged in some private research and that she always needed funds to keep this going. We had no money. Then it came to me how I would help. I got up one morning and said to Roland, 'I'm going to write a book of poems, have them published and sell them in aid of Mrs Bannister's research.'

'Oh great!' he said, 'since when have you been a writer?'

'Since today', I replied. For I knew I would do what I had said. I didn't know how I would do it, mind you – but I knew I would. The poems flowed. I don't know where they came from, and I certainly don't pretend that they are great literature or anything of that sort, but they are heartfelt. I wrote 145 of them in double-quick time. And we did sell them – in little booklets, which we priced at eighty pence.

They must have been readable because I raised £350 which I took to Mrs Bannister at her hospital in Manchester. She and her staff arranged a terrific reception for us and we had a fabulous day out. My happiest memory is of Mrs Bannister – the neurosurgeon – giving the biggest cream cake to Roland – the heart patient!

My appearances in the media were beginning to attract international interest. The press and television media would phone at times which were not always convenient. One morning the American magazine *National Enquirer* phoned and asked me for predictions, just like that, out of the blue. I was a bit snappy with them. I said, 'I'm busy cleaning. Can you ring back tomorrow?' I was surprised by how blasé I had sounded! They did ring again on the following day and I told them that I had seen a vision in which 24 American seamen died on a reconnaissance expedition in the Pacific ocean. Sadly, this occurred eight days later, exactly as I had foreseen it.

It is disconcerting to be asked, at the drop of a hat, to make specific predictions. But the amazing thing is that, when asked, I can usually come up with something. This is never through any striving for results on my part: I am asked and I give.

I find that those who ask do not always take me at my word. Once a man rang and asked airily for some message about the future and I replied, 'There will be a Stock Market Collapse.' I can't remember his exact reply, but it was something like, 'You're joking! Of course it won't collapse!' I was rather niggled by this. I said, 'Look, you've asked me for a prediction, and I've told you: there will be a Stock Market collapse.' And it did collapse. This was October 1987. I have never so much as glanced at a table of stocks and shares in my life.

In that same year I received a very ominous and sombre vision. The atmosphere was melancholy and the outlook threatening. I dreamt I was looking at a group of dignitaries on the steps of a cathedral. They were posed as for a wedding photograph, though I knew that this was not a wedding. The then Archbishop of Canterbury, Dr Robert Runcie, was there. He was standing on the sixth step. Below him, on the bottom step, was his envoy Terry Waite.

Waite turned to the side and walked away from the group. Three days later he was taken hostage in Beirut.

8
...

Breaking Glass, a Deserted Lover and The Marchioness

'Oh, Auntie Barbara, I wish you hadn't told me that! People get very nervous when they hear that they've featured in one of your dreams.' This was my niece, Diane, speaking. I had phoned her to tell her of my dream in which I saw her in great danger from breaking glass.

Diane's father had recently died, and in my dream I saw him holding her hands and smiling in a sort of conservatory. There was an overwhelming sense of danger. Exactly three weeks after this dream, it was Diane's birthday and her husband took her into Beverley to do some shopping. It was a busy Saturday morning in the main shopping centre of the little market town.

Diane likes to look in bookshops and, after a good lunch, this is what she set out to do. There were two bookshops and she stood in the street debating with her husband which one they should try first. They decided on one shop and, while they were browsing (strangely, Diane had picked up a copy of *The Listener*), there occurred a monstrous crashing sound from across the street and a general pandemonium of screams and panic. A horse had got loose and charged through the window of the other bookshop, with the result that fifteen people were badly injured by breaking glass.

My niece is a thoughtful, sensitive person and around this time she had confided in me about one of her last conversations with her father before he died. They were discussing life after death and, to Diane's disappointment, her father said, 'We're just like the flowers of the field – like the daffodils. We come up and have our moment of glory and then we're gone forever.'

This made Diane feel sad. Soon after this conversation, her father died. Then a strange thing happened. Diane's mother returned, bewildered, from a visit to the grave. Some weeks earlier, she had put daffodils on her husband's grave and, although there had been three or four severe frosts, they were still flourishing. This seemed to Diane and her mother to throw fresh light on that last conversation about human life resembling daffodils. Moreover, on the day of Diane's visit to Beverley, there was a charity collection in aid of the Marie Curie Foundation: 'Daffodil Day'. That and the fact that Diane was spared injury in the accident involving glass caused her to ponder once more the mystery of life after death. 'It seemed' she said, 'almost as if my dad had revised his views on the subject!'

I have always believed that my little domestic visions are every bit as significant as the dreams and premonitions which I have about prominent people and affairs. Sometimes the message contained in these close-to-home visions is very cheerful. Oddly enough, I have had more than one such dream concerning Diane and her family.

It was in 1984 when, it seemed, tragedy had struck them. In tears she phoned and told me that her son Philip, aged twelve, had been diagnosed as suffering from the very worst sort of epilepsy. While she was on the telephone I heard myself answer her emphatically, 'No – it isn't severe epilepsy!'

But of course the neurosurgeon was quite certain. He had seen plenty of cases like Philip's before and he said, 'I'm afraid he will never be able to do much for himself.

You'll always have to pick him up from school, and he'll never drive a car.' I was angry at these suggestions and I told my niece that we should light a candle each week and pray that the epilepsy would indeed not be of the severe kind, and that it might go away altogether.

And that is exactly how it turned out. Philip had only one more major seizure and one minor fit. Mr Rawson, the consultant neurosurgeon, called Diane and apologised for his earlier diagnosis. In 1985 – less than a full year later – Philip was taken off medication and has had no further trouble.

There is a follow-up to this story. Some years later, Philip applied for a place at Corpus Christi College, Oxford. Diane said that, unfortunately, he had not been successful and that his name was to be put on the list of general applications for whatever other university places might be available. But I was certain that he would get his place at Oxford, and I said as much. Sure enough, a letter came, just before Christmas, to say that he had made it to Corpus Christi after all.

People have asked me over the years whether I have any other psychological peculiarities. It's a disconcerting question, for I have never considered myself as anything other than completely normal, apart from the premonitions. But these don't change me. I don't turn into something weird or occult just because I experience psychic dreams and visions from time to time. In fact, the occult for its own sake is something which has never held any fascination for me, and in any case it is forbidden territory for a practising Catholic.

But, now I come to think of it, I do have one idiosyncrasy which has been with me from the age of ten: I get by on very little sleep. It all began when I used to do early morning shopping for neighbours during the Depression. There were shortages and queues, and you had to be up early if you wanted to find anything left in the local shops. I used to get up at 5.30 and go and stand in the queue. I did it all through the war as well – I can still see, in my mind's eye, all those propaganda posters on the billboards: *Be Like Dad, Keep Mum* and *Dig For Victory*.

Also, my dad used to get up in the night and listen on the wireless to the World Championship boxing matches from America. I begged to be allowed to get up with him. You should have seen us: father and daughter enjoying midnight – and past midnight – feasts while the rest of the household slept! After these sessions, dad never bothered to go back to bed. He just got his things ready for setting off to work. It was bliss for me to be allowed to stay up! And from that time to this I have never needed more than three or four hours sleep.

By 1989 I was getting used to being asked to appear on television and to speak on radio about my premonitions. There is always a sense of incredulity on the part of the producers and presenters, as if they imagine I'm some sort of trickster. But I cannot manipulate God's universe to suit my personal predictions. All I know is that I have dreams of things to come. And when these turn out to be valid, even the most sceptical of the media people are won over.

In that year, I dreamt that I was looking out of my bedroom window and a van turned up with the name of a television company on the side of it. Three weeks later to the day, that van did arrive – in fading light, just as it had done in my dream – and I was invited to appear on *Look North* in Leeds.

When the day came for my TV appearance, I saw before my eyes the words 'Earthquake' and 'San Andreas'. I told the presenter of the programme that I believed there would be an earthquake in the San Francisco area. This prediction came true and, of course, the date of the television programme is the proof. I can still see Judith Stamper, the presenter, as she turned to the camera after my prediction and said, 'Well, let's hope that's one premonition that doesn't come true!'

But it did. Exactly three weeks later.

I was invited on to a television programme at the Granada studios in Manchester. Because of my psychic experiences, I am always conscious of the fact that there is no real divide between this world and the world to come. As a result of this persuasion, I have got into the habit – nervous and stage-shy person that I am! – of asking the spirit of my father or of our dear daughter Angela to be with me when I know I am to appear on television. We were shown into our room at a splendid Manchester hotel but we soon discovered that there was a fault with the television set. I asked at reception if they would mind sending someone to fix it, but they said it would be easier for us to move to another room. In this second room there was a picture of anemones on the wall – and I have had occasion to refer earlier to the connection between anemones and Angela. But that was not all: on the table in our new room, there was a brief note which read, 'I have cleaned your room, and I hope you find it satisfactory – your maid, Angela.'

The north coast of Devon is one of the most romantic locations in the whole of the British Isles. It resonates with tales of seafaring men and the girls they left behind them; and of course it is Lorna Doone country. Roland and I went on holiday there, taking with us our son Jon, who was about eighteen at the time, and one of his friends. We stayed in a beautiful little cottage.

One night I heard footsteps downstairs, which started to come up the steps. They paused. In the silence I seemed to see a woman reach the top of the stairs, halt briefly in her progress and then turn to go down once again. My son Jon heard the same footsteps. This happened for two nights in succession. I enquired in the village about previous occupants of the house and whether there was any story or legend which might account for what Jon and I had heard.

A neighbour expressed no surprise at all when I told her about the footsteps. She said, 'There was a young woman in the cottage three hundred years ago. She had a lover, but he left her for another. The woman threw herself over the cliff in her distress and she was killed.'

Just as there is no real divide between this world and the world to come, there is no profound separation between past and present, between things which are ancient and things modern. For example, my visions are often accompanied by a flickering like electronic gadgets, light and television sets. This is such a frequent occurrence that I have speculated that perhaps all communication – ancient psychic and modern electronic – uses the same media and forces, only in slightly different ways.

If this is indeed the case, then perhaps it goes some way also to explaining why it is that I seem regularly to foresee events which befall people who make their living by appearing on television – as if, being constantly on screen, the activities of these personalities and entertainers are more susceptible to being picked up by a psychic like myself.

In the late 1980s, I had a very vivid vision concerning an actor who appeared in the television series *The Onedin Line*. He was in a caravan, sitting in his chair, working. Suddenly, he slumped forward and fell. Shortly afterwards, a news item announced that the same actor had died suddenly in the way that I had foreseen. He had been on holiday in a caravan at the time.

Not all of my predictions are of death and destruction by any means. Sometimes they have helped prevent disaster; and as usual, it is the domestic, almost trivial, events which turn out to be the most telling. One afternoon I went to a hairdressing appointment and, before leaving the house, I asked Roland to put a casserole in the oven at a predetermined time. After coming out of the hairdresser's, I went to call on my daughter Sandra. While I was with her, I began to feel uneasy. I knew there was something seriously wrong, but I couldn't pin it down exactly – though I seemed to hear the words: 'A near fire!'

All I knew was that I had to get home quickly. Sandra knew me well enough not to ask too closely of my motives. If I said I had to go, that was good enough for her. She had, after all, grown up accustomed to my psychic awareness. I walked home quickly. As soon as I got inside the house, I could smell something burning. I dashed into the kitchen. There was a tea towel scorching on the oven door. A near fire!

That was, domestically speaking, a near catastrophe averted solely because of my psychic awareness. A domestic delight was Paul moving to set up home with Annetta; but there was a strange occurrence around this event also. The young couple went to live in Gilberdyke, not many miles from Hull, and they invited Roland and me to see their new place.

The night before our visit, I dreamt of their house. It was a neat little place with a white fence around it. When we arrived, I said, 'Oh, but there's no fence!'

'There was, Mum – but it was stolen last night!' said Paul. A trivial event, as I said. But that is how the psychic experience often works. The predictions are not always earth-shaking global catastrophes – though I have seen my share of these – but ordinary, homely happenings of no significance to anyone outside the family. They are no less important for being on a small scale. What, in any case, is an important event? It is not usually something which happens on the grand scale, but more often it is a happening which takes place near at hand and has an effect on people we know and love.

Even the homely visions do not always come at a time which is convenient. Once, on the anniversary of my dad's death, I couldn't sleep, so I went downstairs and began to clean the kitchen. Jon had been out that night and he returned home late. We talked for a while until I felt sleepy. When I returned to bed I was extremely tired and I fell asleep at once. Except I couldn't escape from a message that was imposing itself on my flickering consciousness.

I thought I was hearing my dad's voice. I have long schooled myself to keep a pencil and notepad by the bedside for just this sort of occurrence; but on that particular night I was simply too tired to make much sense of what was being said to me. I actually told my dad to go away! It sounds rude and inhospitable when I recall the incident now. Fancy talking to dad like that! But I was dog tired.

I dropped the pad and the pencil on the floor and fell deeply asleep. In the morning I awoke to discover that I had scrawled: 'Diane. Philip's College. Academics. Travel USA. Fire Escape.' I wrote it out neatly and posted it to my niece. Diane phoned the next day to say that Philip had won a scholarship to go to America, to an institution called Philip's College of Academics. But what about the fire escape? Diane told me that, as my letter arrived through her door, she was reading in *The Observer* newspaper about a new kind of fire escape.

The fire escape had nothing to do with Philip's college; it was just a piece of information that happened to be floating around at the time, and my psychic awareness picked it out. And this illustrates well the nature of my faculty. It is not something which I can control at will. Impressions and sensations of things to come often overtake me entirely unbidden – even when I am falling fast asleep!

Many times I have not welcomed my psychic gift. It is not an entertainment – an interesting phenomenon, like table-rapping, useful only for providing curious people with material for idle chat. Sometimes my visions are not just unwelcome; they are horrific. Perhaps to end this chapter in which I have recounted mainly benign and even mildly humorous episodes I should include three of the most vivid and terrifying of all my visions.

In 1988, I dreamt I was on a beach looking out to sea. I saw a hovercraft. The whole boat seemed to be made of glass, and there was a raging fire within. Children were on the inside hammering on the glass in sheer panic to be let out. Three weeks later, a bus carrying children in France caught fire, and the newsreels described the scene exactly as I had seen it in my dream – children hammering on the windows to be released from the flames.

Why a hovercraft in the dream when in reality the accident had featured a bus? I believe the hovercraft and the sea in my dream symbolised the fact that the incident occurred across the sea. In every other respect, the dream was accurate.

Whenever Roland and I went to Stratford-on-Avon we liked to stay at The Cherry Trees hotel. During one visit we were spending the afternoon in quiet reverie, sitting out in the town square watching the passers-by. We were opposite the theatre. Suddenly I said, 'In half an hour there will be a fire in the theatre and six fire engines will come to deal with it!'

And it happened just as I said. There was a mysterious aspect to this premonition, and I suspect I shall never get to the bottom of it. I saw a man with a briefcase and he went into the theatre just before the fire broke out. I was convinced that he was connected somehow with the cause of the fire. I asked the firemen if this were so, but they would neither confirm nor deny my speculation.

I saw clearly one of the most tragic disasters in modern times. It was 1989 and I dreamt that I was standing on an L-shaped pier. The night was very dark. There appeared a luxury boat full of lights and the sounds of young people enjoying themselves. I could hear the pop of champagne corks. People were laughing and joking. Suddenly I saw the boat sink. I heard the words, 'And they searched all through the night...'

The next day's television news showed searchlights over the water I had seen in my dream. And the newsreader was saying, 'And they searched all through the night...'

This was the sinking of *The Marchioness* on the river Thames.

9
...

From the Sublime to the Ridiculous

In the days before television, the most important events in people's lives were local. There simply wasn't news of far flung places and we were not informed constantly about the economy of Outer Mongolia or of fresh atrocities in parts of Africa. Of course it is a good thing – if often a distressing thing – to know more of what is going on in the world; but it remains true that for most of the hours in each day our most immediate concerns are rightly about what is happening in our own locality.

Our lives are overwhelmingly local, and I believe that this is why many of my premonitions are about events which happen close at hand. Sometimes these events may seem trivial, but really nothing that affects human beings in their daily lives is ever trivial. Our Heavenly Father notices when sparrows fall. The welfare of our family and friends is uppermost in our minds, and this is how it should be. The proper management of our local school and the upkeep of the parish church are matters of great importance. It has been said that worrying about Nicaragua while remaining oblivious to what is going on in your own backyard is a sign of insanity. Certainly, we have a degree of influence over what is taking place in our own neighbourhood, while our effect on world politics tends to be slight.

In this chapter I should like to record a few predictions which were decidedly local. The point is that, though they may be small personal events, they happened; the predictions came true. I do not believe that truth is ever trivial. Also I reckon that it is only to be expected that a psychic person will see things which concern his or her own immediate circle, for this is where his heart is. The psychic gift may be regarded as a treasure. We are told that where our treasure is there shall our heart be as well.

In 1990, I dreamt that I was in a department store. In the corner I could see my daughter-in-law Annetta and her children, Sophie and Damien. Annetta was holding up a bottle of red wine. Sophie looked at the wine and grimaced. I phoned my son Paul, Annetta's husband, the next day and told him the dream.

Paul laughed and said, 'Mother – you and your dreams! Annetta was in a department store the other day and she won six bottles of wine in a competition. She chose red. The sales manager jokingly asked Sophie if she would like to sample the wine. Sophie hates the taste of red wine and so she pulled a face'.

A trivial tale if ever there was one, but it is true; it happened exactly as Paul said and as I dreamt it. But in the same year I had recurring dreams about my grandson James which were anything but trivial. I kept dreaming that I saw him in a derelict landscape. He was running – running away, I would say – down long dark passages, pursued by a large, burly man. I could tell that he was afraid so I told his mother, Sandra, about these nightmares.

Then at the beginning of November, James was on his way from school to his aunt's house. It was dusk, a gloomy late autumn teatime. He took a short cut through some dark passages and he was seized by a huge burly man. James struggled with all his might to escape and, despite his attacker's strength, he got away. He told me afterwards that he was sure he received some sort of spiritual help to evade the evil man's grasp: 'I couldn't have done it on my own, grandma'. I remember James' description of his attacker to the CID: it was an accurate portrait of the man I had seen in those recurring dreams.

Why ever did I dream such a thing? Was it for a warning? I don't know the answer to these questions. All I know – all I ever know – about my premonitions is that they occur and I report them as they happen. Might James have been spared his ordeal if I had warned him, or if his mother had told him of my dream and forbidden him to take that short cut? The puzzling question arises again of whether a premonition can change the future, or whether it can only predict what is going to happen in any case. Is a premonition a warning to take evasive action or is it, as it were, a camera which operates in the future tense? These questions are beyond me: I simply tell what I see and foresee.

On a lighter note I had another dream about James a couple of years later. In real life, he was to go with his school on a skiing holiday in Bulgaria and he was greatly looking forward to it. But I seemed to hear a voice which said, 'No snow! No snow!'

I stuck my neck out and told James, 'You won't be going to Bulgaria.' He contradicted me rather vehemently, but I remained certain that he would not go to Bulgaria. Seven days before the trip was due to begin, it was announced that the destination had been changed to Italy – no snow in Bulgaria! James had told the whole class about my prediction and they can all verify the truth of it. I put the episode in that part of my reminiscences marked Trivial But Amazing.

Just occasionally psychic events occur which go beyond dreaming and clairvoyance and they lead me to use – albeit with great reticence – the word **supernatural**. I am not making this up. I can only tell you exactly what happened and leave you to make up your own mind about it.

Roland and I used to go regularly to my father's grave, which was also the place where my sister Mary who had died as a child and my first daughter Angela are buried. We went to take flowers. That cemetery had been full for a long time and it was all grassed over. There were no tombstones. There were however a small tree by Angela's grave, and we would put our flowers in a niche in this tree. Once on the anniversary of my father's death, I cut two white roses from our garden and took them to the cemetery. My father, Mary and Angela: we were commemorating three relatives. Why did I take only two roses?

An oversight, a lapse of concentration? I don't know. Anyhow, the next time we went to the graves I remembered to cut three flowers. We arrived at the cemetery at 8.45 in the morning. There was no one around. There was never anyone around. As we stepped out of the car, we saw a large blue freesia. I took this flower home. I thought, and I still think, that it was a bloom from heaven. All those years ago, we had placed freesias in my father's coffin.

A sentimental story, perhaps. And I suppose there could have been a natural explanation of the flower. But I have learnt over a lifetime's psychic experiences to understand spiritual atmospheres and nuances, and I firmly believe that the freesia had no natural provenance but that it was meant as a comfort and a reassurance for me. I do not have experiences of this intensity every day or even every year, but I have been given them often enough to recognise their genuineness: I am thinking particularly of the white whirlwind which I saw at the time of Roland's big operation. And as these mysterious events came as a comfort, to me, I pass them on in the hope that they may encourage my readers to know that we are not alone in our troubles and in our distress.

Because of my television appearances and the reporting of my premonitions in the newspapers, I get visitors from time to time who ask me if I have had any vision or dream which might be of some interest to them personally. Well, one night in 1992 I dreamt I was in a hospital car park alone. I saw a lorry which was carrying cylinders of rusted iron or steel. The lorry was reversing towards my car and a girder came right through the windscreen. The dream was so vivid that I ducked in my sleep!

Three weeks later, a lady came to ask whether I had received any premonitions recently. I told her of the car park dream. It had happened to her daughter on the day I dreamt it – exactly as I had seen the events in my vision. The daughter was injured, but I am glad to say that she has made a recovery.

Now for a bit of naughtiness! Another of the ladies who used to come and ask me for predictions arrived and I told her that she would be in a car which would catch fire. It would be a very frightening escapade but, though the car would be a write-off, she and the other person in the car would escape. Three weeks later it happened as I had said it would. The lady came back and breathlessly reported the event but she also begged me not to disclose her identity: she was a married woman and the man with her was her lover.

Sometimes the fact that someone asks me for a premonition is enough to bring one on. I don't know how this works: whether the question stirs up psychic energy or whether it is only the forces of coincidence which are at play. But it has happened again and again. For example, a few years ago I was in a television studio preparing for a programme which Thames Television were making about my predictions.

The researcher, Jane Eames, with whom I had been in conversation said, 'Have you any premonitions today, then?'

Suddenly, I sensed strongly the presence of fire engines and the police and there was the atmosphere of a major incident. Jane said, half-jokingly, 'I hope it's not the studio!' And I replied, also half-jokingly, 'I hope it's not my hotel!' But that night a fire broke out in the kitchen of the hotel where I was staying, and there were great movements of police and firemen just as I had foreseen earlier in the day.

It seems to me that all the varieties of mysterious happenings which I have witnessed in my life are somehow connected. I am certain that there is a spiritual realm. From time to time the veil seems to be lifted – or even only half lifted – and I am given hints and partial revelations of this spiritual reality. Perhaps it is the same spiritual reality which is behind some of the experiences of extra-terrestrial visitations? God the creator of the universe is one, and I believe that his creation is all one piece. The word 'alien' for any creature in God's universe is inappropriate.

This is only speculation on my part, but it seems to fit with an experience which I had in 1995. I dreamt of a Boeing 747 aircraft. There I was on the airfield and the plane was stationary at the edge of the runway. It was lit with an uncanny light, a strange and unearthly luminosity – like fluorescent light. It was a very evocative and emotionally disturbing sight. There were people in the cockpit but not in the passenger section. I said in my dream, 'But it's not on fire!'

Three days later, a Boeing came into Manchester airport and the pilot and co-pilot reported that light had shone in on them so brightly that they had ducked low instinctively. They described how they had been startled by 'an uncanny light'. They were insistent that this light was not from the sun. The passengers had seen nothing of it.

From such a grandiose phenomenon, I come down to earth and record a trivial event which I found amusing at the time. Trivial it may have been, but it certainly happened and it has a strange evocativeness. In March 1995, my friend Peter Mullen came to see me. As soon as he arrived, I had a strong impression of Botany Bay. I could make no sense of this, and neither could Peter. We made the expected jokes about convicts and Australia and I asked Peter whether he was contemplating a period of residence at Her Majesty's pleasure.

Later, when I reflected more seriously on the impression, I wondered if it ought to be interpreted symbolically. I knew for example that Peter had been feeling personally hemmed in by circumstances. Could Botany Bay symbolise a sense of personal restriction? Anyhow, I put it out of my mind.

Three weeks later to the day, Peter was on a journalistic expedition to Tenerife. As his party arrived in Puerto de la Cruz by coach, their guide said to them, 'You will see a great variety of flowers. These beautiful gardens have been here since 1788 and the city is also known as Botanical Bay.'

I can truthfully say that I have received premonitions which have ranged from the sublime to the ridiculous; visions which have moved me to tears of sadness or gratitude, but there have also been dreams so run of the mill as to have been almost banal – comical, to say the least.

I have had ample proof that my dreams and visions are of reality. And reality does not pick and choose which bits of it are deeply serious and which are of little account. Reality, by definition, is of a piece. It is simply the sum total of everything that happens: huge events of earth-shaking significance, but also little domestic doings to which we would hardly give a second thought.

And I am privileged to see some of these happenings out of time, as it were. I do not claim to be able to tell why some events are thus foreseen while others remain hidden to me. I do not know the purpose of these visitations. What I do know is that they happen and I record them exactly as they occur. And the great majority of these premonitions come true just as I originally imagined them.

I am not seeking to convince sceptics or to advance any sort of new explanation of life, the universe and everything. All I can say is that they happen just as I describe them, and they have proved over and over again to contain their own significance and their own fulfilment.

But let Shakespeare have the last word:

'There are more things in heaven and earth, Horatio, than are dreamt of in your philosophy.'

10

A Papal Acknowledgement, a Devastating Fire and a New Home for Sam

One of my proudest possessions is an acknowledgement from Pope John Paul of a volume of my poetry which I sent to the Holy Father in 1987. I was very moved by his declaration that he appreciated their sentiments. Four years later I had an interesting psychic experience connected with a further volume. I dreamt I was at a scrubbed table with my mother. She was holding my hands and repeating again and again, 'It's life; all about life!'

At this time I was gathering together some more of my poems to make another book out of them. I let Father Jenkinson see them – this was three weeks after my dream. It was Sunday evening and I went to church to the Prayer Hour which preceded Benediction. Father Jenkinson was conducting the prayers and he included a poem of mine which happened to be called Life. On the Monday following, I received a request from my publishers Merlin that they be allowed to call the new volume by that title. At once I recalled the dream of my mother and her saying, 'Life, it's all about life!'

This was a small enough event to be sure, but it was significant nonetheless. Certainly it had great emotional and personal significance for me; and it goes to show once again that psychic experiences do not always have to be of world-shaking proportions, but they can also be homely affairs and no less important for that. In fact, I often think that the most telling of all my psychic dreams and visions are not the ones which feature grand public events or international catastrophes, but those that are near to home and which deal with occurrences that would seem quite unremarkable to anyone outside the immediate family circle.

Actually, it is the same with all of us – psychics or not. I mean, ask yourself which events in your life are of the first importance to you. They will not be epics of world history in the making or stuff out of which newspaper headlines are invented. On the contrary, they will be little local difficulties and joys, things that happen in your close circle of friends and kin – literally, familiar things.

The psychic gift does not seem to discriminate between the vast public realm and the small private world where most of us – at any rate, those of us who are not international politicians or movie stars – live, move and have our being. Frequently, my mother features in my visions, and her appearances can be very telling!

For example, in 1992 I dreamt I saw my mother standing with her arms folded. She directed my attention to something that was going on outside the window. I saw a vintage car – a big, shiny, beautiful car it was too. Suddenly, my sister Audrey and her husband Les came into the room. I could read no significance of any kind into this dream. But the next day I learned that Audrey and Les had spent the weekend in Norwich with Les's brother who was a restorer of vintage cars. And another connection: my mother who had appeared in this dream had, in real life, been born in Norwich. A casual, insignificant psychic event?

But nothing that happens to people is ever really

insignificant. I have learned this through all my strange experiences; and of course it is what the Christian faith teaches about our lives here on earth. Besides, I actually find rather reassuring the fact that my psychic gift does not concern itself exclusively with epoch-making events. It would be too much of a good thing, as it were: all forte and no pianissimo makes for tedious music. Because my gift often features mundane events, I understand how real and rooted it is in ordinary, everyday life. If it featured only blockbusting events on the international scale, I would begin to think that the psychic gift itself lacked a sense of proportion.

Still, the dark forebodings are grievous to me and I take no delight in them; and this is what I mean when I repeat that the gift is often a burden – especially when I can do nothing at all to prevent some of the terrible events which I foresee. One of my darkest premonitions occurred at the end of June 1992. I know I shall never be entirely free from the dreadful atmosphere with which it was surrounded.

I dreamt I was in church. I saw a beautiful young woman with long blonde hair. I heard the words, 'So pretty. What a pity you had to die!' Three weeks later we all saw the pictures of Rachel Nickell in the papers – the victim of the Wimbledon Common murder. She was the young woman in my dream. I was certain of it.

There is an even worse certainty connected with this dream – worse because it is so fixed and sure in my mind, but I can do nothing about it. Whenever – even all these years afterwards – I recall the dream of Rachel in the church, I see the man who I am sure was her murderer. He always appears the same to me: he is small, only about five feet six; and he is an athlete with a number on his vest. He is slim, about thirty-one years old and he has receding hair. I know I am not mistaken, for I have had so much experience of telling what accurate and true visions feel like.

After fifty years of my psychic gift, I have at least learned to trust it. But this case makes me feel so powerless. A youngish, slim jogger in a running vest – it's not much for the police to go on, is it? The London parks are full of such men. But I know that this evil man of my vision planned Rachel's murder and that he waited for her to come that way.

As I look back over what I have written in this book, I am startled by the number of times that I have moved house. Roland and I must be the original rolling stones! But in January 1992 we moved to our present house in Warwickshire Close where I think we shall stay. We celebrated our move by asking Father Jenkinson to come and bless the house for us. He did so. And it was he who noticed how rapidly the anemones I planted had grown. These will always be a sign to me of the presence of our dear Angela, the child we lost but who has never seemed far away.

My sister Marjorie came to see us in the new house and I told her that I had had the strangest dream about her and her husband Harry who died in 1979. In this dream, Harry was pointing out Pegasus, the winged horse of the Greek myths, as he flashed across the sky. Why Harry and Pegasus? 'That's easy,' said Marjorie, 'When Harry was in the forces in the Second World War, he had lodged for a time at a house in Ramsgate. This house was called Pegasus and there was a picture of the winged horse on the door post.'

This happened back in 1943 and it illustrates well my claim that the psychic world is not bound by time and space in the ordinary sense. A fifty year old experience – in this case my brother-in-law's war – can come as truly to life as last week, or, as we have seen, next week. We have to live by the ordinary reckoning of time, clock time. But reality is not bound by clock time, and it is the very hallmark of the psychic gift that it moves through the past and the future as if they were aspects of an eternal present. Well, I believe that is exactly what they are.

In fifty years of psychic awareness I have had moments of great exhilaration but also times of near despair. It hurts particularly when people call into question the genuineness of my Catholic faith. 'How can you go along with all that mumbo jumbo and still attend Mass?' I can only reply again that I have never noticed any conflict between the two expressions of spirituality. I did not ask for my psychic gift. It came unbidden and it has stayed with me all my life. My response is simply that spiritual gifts come from God and it is my place to be thankful for what I have been given.

The lovely letter of acknowledgement from the Holy Father was a great comfort to me. I know it was for my poems and not specifically for my premonitions; but really these are two aspects of the same thing. Human personality is not divisible. The Barbara Garwell who writes verse is the same Barbara who receives occasional revelations of the shape of things to come.

I can honestly say that I have never used my psychic gift to anyone's hurt, but always in the interests of trying to be helpful. And I have never tried to make money out of selling predictions or setting myself up as some sort of guru. I have simply recorded what has happened to me and, when people have asked me questions, I have tried to answer as plainly as I can. This book represents my first attempt to take a long look at what has been happening 'in my head' for this last half century.

Happily, every time I have received discouragement and even hostility I have also been given reassurance that my psychic gift is indeed a good thing and nothing to be ashamed of or to try and hide. These reassurances have come at moments in my life which were personally crucial: I am thinking particularly of the many occasions when Roland was extremely ill. I was always given to understand that he would pull through, and this he has done – in spite of tremendous odds against him on more than one occasion. This Roland – who fifteen years ago was given very little hope of survival – last March drove nearly 700 miles on a family holiday in Scotland!

I know that sometimes there is misunderstanding of the nature of psychic gifts, and also we have to face the unfortunate fact that some practitioners are greedy fraudsters who exaggerate their capabilities in order to make themselves rich and who do a lot of harm in the process. But I am not one of these, and I would ask only to be judged by my record as set down in this book of my life.

Just now and again, the psychic gift itself has been an explicit consolation. For example, I have become rather in demand by the media in recent years and in 1994 a television producer asked if he might be allowed to take a picture of me in my Parish Church. I suppose I could have agreed at once and simply taken the producer along to church and let him take the picture then and there – without saying anything to anybody. But that is not my way.

I asked the priest for permission. He said that if it were only up to him I could go ahead without hindrance. But it wasn't, and I must ask the Bishop. So I telephoned the Bishop's office and I was surprised and disappointed when he asked me to wait for a decision: he promised to get back to me with his answer, but – for whatever reason – he did not do this. Not even after I had reminded him that I have been a member of the congregation for 60 years and that I wasn't about to do anything untoward in the Church, but merely have my picture taken there.

I don't blame the Bishop. I am sure he always acts for

the best reasons and perhaps, as an ordinary layperson, I am not aware of all the ecclesiastical niceties. But his response hurt and I can't pretend it didn't. But the day after my phone call to the Bishop and its disappointing outcome, I received in the post from a friend a picture of the Lord Jesus: and in this picture He was also standing outside the church door! My friend had known nothing of my request to the Bishop, so her sending the picture of Our Lord was entirely out of the blue and coincidental – or was it?

My interpretation of the event is that God is with me in my gift even if representatives of the Church cannot always express their wholehearted support.

One summer Friday in 1994, I went to a DIY warehouse in Hull to buy some wood for a job about the house. I saw a saleslady called Denise but they didn't have the wood which I required. Roland and I took the opportunity to ask about conservatories, and I recall we had quite a long conversation about connecting doors. Denise said, 'We can sort it all out next Friday.'

The following Tuesday, I dreamt of a huge, violently hot warehouse and I was anxiously trying to find a cool spot. There was no furniture in the place, but everywhere hundreds of people in a blind panic. I saw a woman on a rostrum. She was very striking in appearance, with attractive fair hair. It was Denise from my Friday meeting. I made my way to the doors from where I could tell that it was a brilliantly sunlit day and so very hot. But I couldn't get out.

As I looked up into the sky, I saw what looked like a huge black animal – scaly, like an endless snake or else a dinosaur. At this moment I awoke.

Later, wide awake and sitting in my own front room, I saw a vision of a firedoor. On the Friday morning I was ironing at my daughter's house when I saw the firedoor again. I knew there would be a fire in Hull, but for some reason I had not made the connection with the DIY warehouse.

Roland came to collect me at lunchtime and it was then that we heard Denise's voice on the car radio talking about a disastrous blaze at the warehouse. I looked into the sky and there was a long plume of smoke exactly like the black snake of my dream. The fire, having occurred during shopping hours, had caused a great deal of panic, as I had seen in my dream. The store was burned down, but luckily no one was hurt or trapped in the inferno.

That was an event on the grand scale, but I am frequently amazed and amused by the realisation that no event seems to be too modest to feature in a psychic vision. In 1994, for instance, we suffered a domestic sadness – and its joyful sequel – which was prefigured by one of my dreams. I dreamt I was in a sectioned-off place – something like public toilets. I was obliged to walk through these buildings and this was distasteful to me because the floors were caked with excrement. I awoke saying out loud, 'We call him Sam!'

Three weeks later our dog, Ben, was run over and killed. I was distraught. The vet advised me to go and look around the kennels at the stray dogs. When I arrived I remembered my dream at once, because the place was in a similarly dirty condition. It was there that I saw a lovely little dog, all affectionate life and fun. The keeper of the kennels said, 'We call him Sam!'

Sam now lives at home with Roland and me.

11
...

Thank You Barbara!

Why should I blow my own trumpet when I can find so many people who are more than willing to do this for me! Seriously though, I should like to include just a selection from the great number of people who have written to me over the years to thank me for helping them with my predictions. So I shall say no more now, but simply allow the testimonials to speak for themselves.

To the Producer, *Out Of This World*,
Watching *Out Of This World* last Friday, I immediately recognised Mrs Barbara Garwell. A few years ago, my partner John Horsman and I visited Mrs Garwell at her then home in Aldbrough. I used to live nearby at Mappleton.

John and I have been together for ten years and for quite a number of those years we wanted to start a family together, but, because of various problems, it just didn't happen and we began to think it was hopeless. However, Mrs Garwell told us that we would have a baby girl. Still nothing happened.

Then in 1992 I did get pregnant, but sadly I suffered a miscarriage; and four months later the same thing happened again. Though very upset, at least now we knew it was possible; and in September 1993 I found I was pregnant again. We were delighted and terrified at the same time. But always at the back of my mind were

Mrs Garwell's words, and I began to let myself believe that this time would be OK.

Mrs Garwell had told us that many of her predictions have been recorded and verified. The pregnancy progressed and because I was then forty-one the consultant advised an amniocentesis – as a blood test had shown that the child could be at risk of being a Down's Syndrome baby. But because of Mrs Garwell's words I refused the test as I just knew that whatever happened this would be our baby girl, and that she was meant to be ours.

On 7th June 1994, Rachel Phoebe arrived with difficulty, bruised and battered – but beautiful! We knew Mrs Garwell had moved house, but not her new address. We are delighted to be able to confirm another prediction for her.

This was not all. Mrs Garwell also told us that some friends of ours would go to America; and this they did. She also told us that we would get the details of a house in the post in a big white envelope. The next day, the confirmation of our holiday booking arrived – in a big white envelope!

So Mrs Garwell, thank you for giving us the hope and strength to carry on. We got our reward eventually, and Alison – my daughter who is nearly sixteen – got her little sister at last!

Can I just add that through it all, Mrs Garwell said that, after the tears, the sun would shine again. This little thought always made me feel better and, at low times, it still does.

Yours sincerely,
Rita Beadle

To whom it may concern,
Barbara has rung me about things connected to my life
and to the lives of my family and friends. Some of these
things happen at once and others take rather longer. She
once told me that a lens would fall out of my spectacles
and I had to get new frames in a hurry as I need them for
reading.

Barbara said I mustn't be talked into expensive frames.
I wasn't!

Yours faithfully,
Marjorie Cooper

Dear Barbara,
Thank you for your recent reading. It has correctly
predicted the future concerning myself in three distinct
areas:
  (i) My pregnancy – baby due in May.
  (ii) You were right about the change of
       employment for my husband.
  (iii) And yes, we did have problems with our
       plumbing – just as you said we would!

Yours sincerely,
Joanne Hoggard

...I had the pleasure of meeting Barbara Garwell some
years ago when during times of great personal distress
I went to have a reading with her.

I saw an article in the *Hull Daily Mail* which gave an
account of her dreams and the help she had given to so
many people. The comfort and help she gave me was
wonderful. Now when I have any problems, it is to
Barbara I go. She also gave me a book of poems which
she had written, and I found these to be very comforting
as well.

I. M. Watson (Mrs)

To whom it may concern,
Barbara told me that one day I would have a lock-up
shop. She asked me if I had any dealings with a butcher.
I didn't know any butchers and I was certainly not
thinking of buying a lock-up shop! Two years later,
I took an empty shop with my partner, Sandra, and the
landlord is a butcher. It used to be a butcher's shop.

She told me that I would find myself filling in forms to
an insurance company and that a surveyor would come
round to the house. When we'd been away and left the
eldest girls alone, they had a party at which, without their
knowing, someone had burnt the cushion on the new
settee. A surveyor came round. I filled in forms to obtain
the settlement...

My brother was going to phone, Barbara said, with
news that a sister-in-law would not live long. Sadly, this
came true a month later when my brother rang to give me
news of his wife who died a week after his phone call.

Barbara once told me to collect a chain from the
jewellers as my aunt had left it to me in her will. She
could have got this information from no-one, but it
turned out to be exactly as she had said...

Barbara said we would be changing our car from a
grey one to a blue one. Later we did change the car, but,
as I thought from the look of it, to a silver one. On
inspecting the log book, though, I saw that in fact it was
registered as blue...

A. Phillips (Mrs)

To whom it may concern,
I have known Barbara Garwell for about ten years and
once during this time she told me not to go to Scunthorpe
on a special journey in a blue car. I was subsequently
offered two lifts in blue cars, and I refused them in the
light of what Barbara had said. One of these cars broke

down, burst into flames and blew up...

She also told me that someone close to me in the family would become very ill and have to be hospitalised on a number of occasions over many years, but that eventually they would make a recovery. This person is now better after eight years' illness.

B. Kirkby (Mrs)

To whom it may concern,
Having known Barbara for a few years, I find her to be exceptionally honest and accurate in her knowledge of the spiritual world and in what the future holds for me.

Being a bit of a sceptical person, I was apprehensive on my first visit but Barbara's predictions and guidance have helped me enormously in my personal and business life. She has helped me make decisions that have greatly improved my business – going from a small shop to having multiple shops in the city centre. I have often consulted Barbara on numerous occasions. In my personal life Barbara has mentioned people who have passed over to the spiritual world and she even named one in particular who I was very close to.

When she mentioned him, I could actually smell the tobacco from the pipe which he used to smoke!

If I need to make any difficult decisions in the future, I will continue to consult Barbara before committing myself to any new venture; and I would highly recommend her to anyone.

Anita Harman (Mrs)

To whom it may concern,
I have visited Barbara Garwell many times over the past few years.

On my visits to her, she told me many things including how my father died ten years before; also that he had worked in Saudi Arabia. She also told me that I would have a house built somewhere where there was a lot of white powder covering it. I then bought a plot of land near Beverley and it turned out there used to be a chalk pit across the main road from it.

She also told me I would have a baby within two to five years. I was never the maternal type, and I never wanted children; yet just over two years later I became pregnant with my son.

I visited her a year ago and she told me there would be a major break-up in my relationship and that there would be a reconciliation – but only if I wanted it. She also told me there was a gentleman on the horizon, between forty and forty-four years old. I thought she was trying to cheer me up at the time; and yet when my ex-fiancé begged to come back I would not let him because I am now in a very happy relationship with a man of forty-two years!

I have been to various card-readers and psychics over the years, and most of them tell you the old stories of getting married, having children and being happy. I must say that Barbara is very different from anyone I have ever visited. She goes into such detail and it is all so accurate that it is uncanny.

Every time I have visited Barbara I have written down all the details and over the months I have referred back to them. I have found that Barbara is least 85–90% accurate. There is no way she could have known anything about me, or about anyone connected with me, and yet she seems to know so much!

I intend to carry on visiting Barbara for many years to come, because I am fascinated and intrigued by the way she gets so many things just right – and also because she is such a nice, genuine person.

Wendy Kelly

To whom it may concern...
When I first heard about Barbara, I must admit to feeling very sceptical. I felt that people who read cards either tell you bad news or pretend to read your mind. Barbara does neither of these things.

I was talking to her one sunny morning when, suddenly in the middle of the conversation, she asked, 'Who do you know with a badly-marked face – someone with acne?' I told her it would be a friend of my husband's – someone we hadn't seen for at least ten years, and we no longer knew where he was living. 'You will hear something about him very soon,' was Barbara's reply.

The following day, my husband and I went to a Spring Fair where we were on duty with the St John's Ambulance Brigade. During the afternoon, we met the friend with the marked face.

On another occasion, Barbara was convinced that I had connections with Leeds. I said this was not the case, but she replied, 'Ask your family'. I asked my aunt about Leeds. It turned out that my great grandfather had lived there near Armley Jail.

Barbara also said my mother was musical, that there would be another grandchild who would be left-handed and that he would have something in common with my mother; moreover that they would write sheet music together. This all came true.

There were many other things: for example, a man with an accordion at a white cottage – this was my mother's cousin. There were many other revelations. One thing I know for certain: Barbara knew things about me that I myself didn't know at the time and which I could not have known.

Elizabeth Henellye

To whom it may concern...

I am Barbara Garwell's eldest niece and throughout my life I have been aware of my aunt's psychic ability. An interesting example of this occurred on the evening of 11th September 1989.

I belong to a women's discussion group and I had invited Barbara to tell us of her dreams and premonitions. In the middle of her recollections, she suddenly stopped and remarked that there was a blue car suspended over the head of Jill, one of our members. This phenomenon continued throughout the evening and caused some puzzled amusement.

Barbara said that the car was either sky blue or else metallic blue. Jill concluded that it must be the blue Mini which she had once owned in 1964. At half past ten we were about to leave when Barbara remarked that the back side window of the envisioned car was now smashed. She said, 'The shattered glass looks like a spider's web.'

The following day Jill's son rang her to say that his car had been broken into the previous evening and that the back side window had been smashed! An astonished Jill explained to her son the events of the previous evening, concluding with the words, 'And the shattered glass looked like a spider's web.'

'Yes, Mum,' said Phil 'that is exactly how I would describe it.' Phil's car was a blue metallic colour.

Diane Wells

Dear Barbara,

I am compelled to write to you to say how much I appreciate all your invaluable help during the past six years when you have been undertaking my readings.

You have transformed my life with perceptions and recommendations, guiding me through many a sticky situation. You pin-pointed my way through a problem which appeared insurmountable at the time. Your ability calmly to sense a way through troubled waters has always exceeded my expectations of a mere mortal.

You have always given me confidence by your interpretation of life ahead to develop my potential. I would never have done this without your help. Your integrity and expert judgement are beyond reproach. Your visions have undoubtedly proved correct at all times, even though I must admit there have been occasions when I found it difficult to believe...Many a time I have quietly said to myself, 'Sorry, Barbara for disbelieving you' – because what you predicted always came true sooner or later.

You are a real lady with a genuine fondness for the human race. You give of your time and your gift to many grateful people. Thank you, Barbara: you deliver the goods!

Carol

To whom it may concern...
I have known Barbara since about 1980. I met her after she had contacted me about her premonitions. I made a thorough study of her premonitions over several years and interviewed her, the family and witnesses. I wrote and published two scientific papers on my investigation of Barbara:

  (i) Hearne, K.M.T. (1982) 'Three cases of ostensible premonition from a single percipient'. *Journal of the Society of Psychical Research*, 51 (791):288–291.

  (ii) Hearne, K.M.T. (1986) 'An analysis of premonitions deposited over one year from an apparently gifted subject'. *JSPR*, 53 (804):376–382.

In addition I wrote about her in a chapter on gifted percipients in my book *Visions of the Future* (Aquarian Press 1989).

We have appeared together on various TV and radio programmes to discuss her premonitions.

Barbara Garwell is a very honest, humble and straight-forward person who possesses a fascinating ability to foresee unexpected future events. She also seems to have a powerful psychic ability in areas of telepathy and clair-voyance. Several incidents spring to mind.

For instance, when talking about a recent girlfriend of mine, Barbara insisted that something was wrong with one of her eyes. (I had certainly not discussed this woman with Barbara before.) It took me a few seconds to remember that indeed the girlfriend did have a condition (Adey's Sign) that meant that one pupil was larger than the other.

As another example, Barbara told me after we met that she saw me conducting music. In recent years I have taken up composition and a Requiem by me is being recorded on CD. I have also completed a musical. It is very likely that I shall be conducting my music publicly in the near future.

I unhesitatingly approve of a book being written specifically about Barbara and her amazing cases of fore-sight. People with abilities such as hers can help theorists to change our whole concept of the nature of the universe.

Keith Hearne BSc; MSc; PhD (Psychologist)

12
...

Towards the New Millennium

And so I come to the last chapter which will be the shortest of all in length but which may turn out to be the most significant of them all. For I should like to set down here some of the events which I believe I now foresee for 1996 and the years beyond.

I must add a cautionary note. Readers who have got this far in my book will know that my premonitions tend to come true after three days or three weeks. As I write this chapter, however, and because of the practicalities which attend the printing of a book, I am having to cast my imagination further than usual into the future. All the predictions which follow were made in the early months of 1995.

1. I see members of the Royal Family in danger at sea.
2. There will be a time of political upheaval and uncertainty and perhaps a coalition government in the UK. This I sense strongly as occurring around April 1996.
3. I feel I should offer my apologies to someone for foreseeing a fat man as the next British Prime Minister!
4. Around 1 June 1996, I see a programme of re-armament in the UK in which many new tanks are to be built.
5. I fear for a dangerous new involvement between

the USA and Russia, and this may even come to war.

6. There will be much new drilling for oil, but also an oil rig explosion in the far east.
7. A large British airport will be closed.
8. An important breakthrough in the treatment of diabetes.
9. Princess Diana is to have a daughter.
10. The Conservative government will be defeated.
11. Prince Philip will suffer an illness.
12. There will be the tragic loss of a spaceship – perhaps the space shuttle.
13. A prominent person in American public life will be assassinated.
14. Some dramatic news concerning the British showjumper Harvey Smith.
15. An explosion in the North Sea.
16. The fraud squad will be called to investigate the British Government.
17. An important British naval vessel will be lost.
18. Something serious connected with the Canadian Pacific Railway.
19. There will be a big shooting incident in Australia.
20. The election of a new Pope likely in March 1996.
21. Dramatic news about the great blue whale.
22. There will be substantial changes in the organisation of the British police force with perhaps a reduction in the age of permitted recruitment and there will be fewer police cars.
23. A large prison – Wormwood Scrubs? – to close.
24. A break-in at Buckingham Palace.
25. Some important news of a Swedish princess.
26. There will be a violent accident on the Isle of Man – possibly in the TT race.

27. Serious troubles in Indonesia.
28. The sinking of a luxury liner.
29. A moving story concerning Harry Secombe.
30. Saddam Hussein in the world headlines again.